New Deal Fat Cats

NEW DEAL
FAT CATS

Business, Labor, and Campaign Finance
in the 1936 Presidential Election

MICHAEL J. WEBBER

FORDHAM UNIVERSITY PRESS
New York
2000

Library of Congress Cataloging-in-Publication Data

Webber, Michael J.
    New Deal fat cats : business, labor, and campaign finance in the
1936 presidential   election / Michael J. Webber.—1st ed.
        p.   cm.
    Includes bibliographical references and index.
    ISBN 0-8232-1946-1 (hc)—ISBN 0-8232-1947-X (pbk)
        1. Presidents—United States—Election—1936.   2. Campaign
funds—United States.   I. Title.
JK526 1936
327.7′8′097309043—dc21   99-048262

Printed in the United States of America
00 01 02 03 04   5 4 3 2 1
First Edition

For Mam, Dad, and Ian

CONTENTS

TABLES

ACKNOWLEDGMENTS

My fascination with American politics and history began as an undergraduate at the University College of Wales, Aberystwyth, where Michael Foley's seminars on various aspects of American government and society caused me to put aside more enervating undergraduate pursuits in favor of studying. Little did I realize that years later, after a circuitous journey of working in English heavy industry and Welsh horticulture, my interest in American politics would be rekindled at the University of California, Santa Cruz under the skilled mentorship of Bill Domhoff. I have, therefore, had the enormous good fortune to learn about American politics from some of its leading academic practitioners in two of the most beautiful places on earth.

In the course of researching and writing this book, numerous people have helped me, and I have incurred many debts, which are far easier to acknowledge than to discharge. By far, my biggest debt is to Bill Domhoff, a superb teacher, colleague, and friend who has supported and encouraged me at every stage of my career. As a sociologist, his passion for good ideas has been an inspiration and his concern for intellectual craftsmanship a model to emulate. In particular, I would like to thank him for his critical, insightful, and detailed comments on various drafts of the manuscript, his help and advice with the statistical parts of the analysis, and his gentle prodding and steady encouragement while I was writing.

The project was initially facilitated through the kindness of Herbert Alexander of the Citizens Research Foundation at the University of Southern California, who made available to me much of the campaign finance data for 1936. Research money from the Faculty Development Funds at the University of San Francisco enabled me to travel to the National Archives in Washington D.C. in order to examine their collections on the presidential elections held during the New Deal years. Robert Bulman,

Kerri Brady, Sanae Suzuki, Violette Jara-Rodriguez, and George Parker have all provided valuable research assistance at different stages of the project. My thanks also go to Mary Bea Schulte at Fordham University Press for her patience and support.

My friends and colleagues at the University of San Francisco have created a wonderfully supportive environment in which to work, and my thanks go to Andrew Goodwin, Esther Madriz, Anne Roschelle, Marie Baillargeon, Laleh Shahideh, Becky King, Lois Lorentzen, Mike Stanfield, Bill Edwards, Karin Bouwer, Nancy Campagna, Gerardo Marin, and Stanley Nel. In addition, Jennifer Turpin and Robert Elias were key figures in getting me started on this book, and they made a number of very helpful suggestions at an early stage. Scholarly contributions aside, their friendship and encouragement were even more important in bringing this project to completion.

For much of the time, I live with one foot in the United States and the other in my native Wales. Traversing cultures and boundaries can be painful as well as exciting, but one of its great virtues is being able to observe first hand how loving, generous, and compassionate people can be, no matter where they are from. In the United States, there are many people to thank, but Marina, Bristow, Isabel, Scott, Wendy, Tim, Holly, Donna, Susan, Kyle, Michael, and Gary deserve particular mention. Nick Vecchione of course provided abuse, support, blandishment, conversation, and humor in equal measure—all delivered with great affection. My special thanks go to Mary and Anna Linduska. In Wales, many friends were a constant source of strength despite my long absences and infrequent correspondence. Time and distance has not dulled my affection for them, so to Beverley, Sian, Roland, Debbie, Neil, Dave, and Shelley, *diolch yn fawr*.

Finally, the best part of finishing this book is that it gives me the opportunity to express my gratitude for all the love and support I have received from my family: from my parents, Delphine and John Webber, and my brother, Ian; and from Sharon, Carole, Dennis, Stephen, and David; and also from those whom I can no longer thank in person but who have nonetheless left their mark on my life. Whatever I have accomplished is because of them.

New Deal Fat Cats

1

The New Deal in Historical and Theoretical Perspective

The New Deal has been a major topic of scholarly debate for historians, political scientists, and economists for many years. More recently, it has interested sociologists who are concerned with the nature of political power in capitalist states. This concern has manifested itself in contentious debates over the degree of business influence on key New Deal legislation such as National Industrial Recovery Act, Agricultural Adjustment Act, Social Security Act, and National Labor Relations Act and on the subsequent establishment and expansion of such state agencies as the National Recovery Administration, Social Security Administration, and U.S. Department of Agriculture. Although ostensibly focused on questions of policy formation and state institutional development, these debates have turned the politics of the New Deal into an important arena wherein competing theories of the state are contested and arbitrated. This has revealed wide theoretical differences among pluralists (e.g., Schlesinger 1960), neo-Marxists (e.g., Quadagno 1984, 1988; Jenkins and Brents 1989), state autonomy theorists (e.g., Skocpol 1980; Finegold and Skocpol 1995), and non-Marxist class-dominance theorists (e.g., Domhoff 1990, 1996).

Although the literature has burgeoned on class conflict, the rise of labor unions, and the degree to which legislation and state institutions favor capital or labor, nonetheless the relationship between business, organized labor, and political parties during the New Deal has received relatively scant attention. This oversight is curious in light of the coverage now given to the role of business leaders and organized labor in financing election campaigns. Through a detailed examination of campaign finance in the

1936 presidential election, this book takes a closer look at the relationship between business, labor, and political parties during the New Deal. After reviewing all the major claims concerning financial support given by business and labor to the two dominant parties during this election, the study analyzes the actual class basis and social composition of these contributions. By providing a historically grounded, sociological explanation of a crucial period in American political life, I will shed light on key theoretical questions concerning the two-party system in the United States, the character of the capitalist class, the importance of organized labor, and the nature of the state.

THE STATE OR CAPITAL: WHO GOVERNED DURING THE NEW DEAL?

Social scientists have used various theoretical perspectives to explain the politics and policies of the New Deal. The conventional and often dominant wisdom on the power of business can be found within pluralist theory (for an overview see Carnoy 1984:10–43; Alford and Friedland 1985:35–158; Finegold and Skocpol 1995:157–65). Business is seen as only one special interest group among many because power is dispersed among various groups with heterogeneous interests and resources. With the state acting as a neutral arbitrator, other well-organized groups (such as labor unions and citizen groups) can compete equally with business. However, because business groups are sometimes divided among themselves, other interest groups may occasionally come together to defeat them. As a result, business is sometimes forced into making coalitions with other interest groups.

Because power is diffused throughout society, and the fragmented nature of business interests makes unified political action difficult, pluralists do not believe that capitalists are capable of acting as a ruling class. Mainstream historical debates on the New Deal have echoed these assumptions, focusing on how new, well-organized interest groups—most notably organized labor—were able to secure a place in the political system, at least in part as a result of divisions among capitalists (see Degler 1959; Dahl 1961; Leuchtenburg 1963; Rose 1967; Truman 1971; Lindblom 1977).

State autonomy theorists posit an alternative approach to the

New Deal. They see the state as a potentially autonomous organizational actor possessing the ability to impose its own political and policy objectives on society, independently of actors and groups in civil society (see, for example, Skocpol 1980; Skocpol and Ikenberry 1983; Skocpol and Amenta 1985; Finegold and Skocpol 1995). The actual exercise of this autonomy depends upon the fiscal resources, coercive power, and administrative capacity of the state, all of which are normally aimed at maintaining domestic order and national defense (Barrows 1993:127).

State managers make policy by drawing heavily on technical experts and intellectuals. Although these managers ensure that capital accumulation is secure in order to maximize state revenues, acute domestic and international crises may force them to act against dominant class interests to restore domestic harmony and protect national security. Institutional development is also crucial because the state must have the administrative and bureaucratic capacity to carry out its policy objectives (Barrows 1993:134; Finegold and Skocpol 1995:50–65). Within this perspective, empirical studies of the New Deal by state autonomy theorists have stressed the variability in autonomy due to the fragmented nature of state institutions and the unevenness of administrative structures across policy sectors (Skocpol 1980; Skocpol and Finegold 1982, 1990; Skocpol and Amenta 1985; Finegold and Skocpol 1995).

State-centered accounts of the New Deal have been challenged, especially by those working within a Marxist framework, but Marxist analyses of the relationship between class structure and the state have crystallized around two different theories of the state (Held 1984:31–39). From the instrumentalist perspective the state serves the interests of a united capitalist class at the expense of all other groups in society. With superior economic resources and access to government bureaucrats, and given the ruling-class background of many senior state officials, the capitalist class prevails on virtually all major issues. Instrumentalists argue that without business support, many of the New Deal's liberal reforms would not have been enacted into law (Jessop 1990:144–69; Barrows 1993:13–50; Finegold and Skocpol 1995:176–77).

Unlike the instrumental Marxists, structural Marxists argue that the state is relatively autonomous from class interests. It disorganizes and fragments the working class while pursuing policies necessary for capital accumulation, even when those policies antagonize particular segments or fractions of the dominant class. In later formulations, the state was considered an arena of class struggle as it displaced conflict from the economic to the political sphere through ideology, individualization of workers, coercive use of law, and artificial claims to national identity (Carnoy 1984:97–121; Jessop 1990:61–72). This view underscores a number of Marxist accounts of the New Deal where it is argued that because capitalists had a narrow view of their own interests, the state "put into motion plans for economic recovery that represented the compromise not only between capital and labor but also within capital itself" (Levine 1988:172–73). Other structuralists have emphasized such factors as the conflict between segments of monopoly and nonmonopoly capital; the resolution of disputes within the state in favor of future accumulation needs of capital; and the linking of emergent state structures to class interests (Quadagno 1984; Gilbert and Howe 1991).

None of these general theoretical perspectives is without its problems. Pluralists overlook the evidence indicating that power is not as widely distributed as they assume. The disproportionate economic and political power enjoyed by business means that business rarely loses on issues it regards as important—particularly labor policy, taxation, and economic regulation. Furthermore, business is capable of unified class action even though conflict between rival class segments may mean that it does not prevail on every issue.

State autonomy theorists have had problems establishing when and to what degree the U.S. state is autonomous because its fragmented constitutional and administrative structure makes it susceptible to domination by society-centered interests. Moreover, trying to clarify the ambiguous boundaries between state and civil society is difficult, particularly within the attempt to assess administrative capacity and to specify the role of technical experts (e.g., Cammack 1989:278; Mitchell 1991:77–96; Barrows 1993:142–44).

Within the Marxist camp, instrumentalism has often been castigated as being little more than a conspiracy theory. Rival theorists have been critical of its alleged focus on the class background, motivation, and conduct of individual state actors rather than on the structural economic forces making up the capitalist state. Furthermore, instrumentalists are said to have a hard time explaining why capitalists would engage in any form of political mobilization given that their control of the state seems so complete (van den Berg 1988:221–40; Himmelstein 1990:152–64; Barrows 1993:45–50). Structuralism, on the other hand, has been roundly criticized for its deterministic and functionalist logic. The state's actions to secure capital accumulation are developed independently of the content of state policy and the consequences of political conflict. Thus there are problems in identifying which needs are functional for capital accumulation and which state policies meet those needs, especially because "most apparatuses consist of several institutions and most institutions are multifunctional" (Barrows 1993:71).

Class-dominance theory provides a more nuanced way of looking at New Deal politics, avoiding many of the theoretical pitfalls outlined above. Working from detailed case studies within power structure research, class-dominance theorists synthesize elements of the class and organizational perspectives to demonstrate the existence of a power elite, which is both a social upper class and a ruling class. The power elite is, in effect, a leadership group in a segmented dominant class (Domhoff 1990:17–28, 38–39; 1996:7–50; 1998:9–28, 286–289). Essentially, class-dominance theory attempts to show that there is "(1) a small social upper class (2) rooted in the ownership and control of a corporate community that (3) is integrated with a policy-planning network and (4) has great political power in both political parties and dominates the federal government in Washington" (Domhoff 1996:18). The power elite is not completely monolithic, nor does its power go wholly unchallenged. Rival segments of the capitalist class have disagreements with one another, and because different segments are said to control the Democratic and Republican parties, these disputes manifest themselves in political conflict. Furthermore, marginalized and exploited groups are not totally powerless—they occasionally exert enough pressure to force concessions from the power elite or take advantage of divisions between rival segments of the capitalist class. This is particularly the case for the liberal-labor coalition that emerged within the Democratic Party during Roosevelt's first term. Class-dominance theory thus takes class conflict seriously while recognizing the importance of noneconomic conflicts, particularly around race, ethnicity, and religion.

Although class-dominance theorists give great analytical weight to the ownership of capital, they also emphasize the way various corporate and state institutions regularize the patterned and unequal distribution of resources typical of capitalist societies (Barrows 1993:14). Most important, "the institutional structures of the state can condition the way in which political power is exercised and organized in the United States" (Domhoff 1998:11). Political institutions and processes assume great importance in class-dominance theory, and it is within this context that the study of political parties and campaign finance becomes significant.

This is especially true of the United States, where the existence of even limited democracy is a constant threat to the prerogatives of capital because groups outside the power structure (organized labor and racial and ethnic minorities in particular) always have the potential to seize control of various agencies of the state and initiate policies antithetical to capital accumulation. The reasons why this potential has gone unrealized are many and complex, but any credible explanation has to include the workings of the American party system where plurality, not majority voting, together with single member districts, have produced a "winner-take-all," two-party system. This renders third party challenges difficult (if not impossible) while encouraging the formation of pre-election coalitions that obscure party differences in order to gather as much electoral support as possible (Rosenstone, Behr, and Lazarus 1984:16–47; Domhoff 1990:229–32; 1996:40–50; 1998:204–6).

The end result of the state system created in the course of American history is that elections matter. They provide a mechanism by which rival class segments can settle their disputes, while also giving ordinary people a limited political voice in deciding which class segment will rule. They also allow for democratic input on policy decisions—especially in times of social and political unrest (Domhoff 1998:207–8). But elections require money. This is particularly so in a political system in which candidates are forced to blur policy preferences to build winning coalitions—

resulting in campaigns that stress individual personality and name recognition. In these circumstances, many candidates are at the mercy of big campaign contributors—mostly from the dominant class. Large contributions can also come from organized labor, as happened for the first time in the 1936 election. The major exception to the general need for large donations in the 1936 presidential election was the South, where a large percentage of low-income people were excluded from voting, and middle-income and wealthy voters were overwhelmingly Democratic.

MONEY AND MOTIVE:
CAMPAIGN FINANCE AS AN INDICATOR OF POWER

Money is essential to political campaigns. However, although a certain large minimum is usually necessary to mount a campaign (making support from wealthy donors indispensable), the campaign with the most money does not always win (Heard 1962:34). In 1936, for instance, the Republicans spent $8.8 million compared to $5.1 million for the Democrats, but the Democrats won the presidential election with 62.5 percent of the two-party vote nationally (Overacker 1937:476; Nie, Verba, and Petrocik 1979:75).

Although dollar amounts are interesting and useful, for the purposes of this book, individual campaign finance contributions are a much more important indicator of different business and labor leaders' political preferences. Money, as Herbert Alexander observed, "is only symbolic of other political goals" (1972:11). The real objective of politics is power; money is merely an instrument for gaining access, achieving influence, or obtaining other resources in the political system. Indeed, as Alexander has suggested, "Because of its universality, money is a tracer element in the political process, marking the tracks both of the individual or group seeking influence and of the candidate and the party seeking election to office. Revelations of their transactions and associated behavior deepens understanding of the flows of influence and power" (1972:11). Other commentators have gone further than this. Mills (1956) argued that money is the mechanism by which economic power is translated into political influence, while Domhoff (1998) suggests that wealthy individuals exercise an inordinate influence on the electoral process through their donations. With regard to presidential politics, Lundberg (1937) and Allen (1987; 1991; with Broyles 1989) have shown how personal fortunes have an enormous impact on electoral outcomes.

Campaign donations can, therefore, act as an important "tracer element," marking the tracks of business and labor influence in the political system. Given the power of business in American society, it would be naive to argue that campaign contributions constitute the only mechanism by which business seeks to secure its interests, because campaign donations are "backed by the wider range of business power and influence" (Clawson, Neustadtl, and Scott 1992:22). But in a formally open democratic system, business cannot risk being crippled by a government dominated by groups hostile to its interests. Resources must be devoted to the political interests of business, and contributions to political campaigns are a crucial element of its broader political strategy (25).

Skeptics might argue that the concept of "business interests" involves an excessive degree of reification and may be problematic when drawing inferences about corporate behavior from individual campaign contributions. Many contemporary analysts of business political behavior, however, have argued that a firm's interests can be identified as the interests of those who control the firm and set its long-term corporate policy—namely the board of directors (Useem 1984; Mintz and Schwartz 1985; Mizruchi 1992). The assumption here is that similar behavior is a function of similar structural position (Mizruchi 1992:51). Such an assumption has a long sociological pedigree. Max Weber defined a corporate organization as an "aggregative social relationship" and located its governing authority in an "administrative staff" committed to the goals of the organization (Weber 1993:115). Weber explicitly stated that a board of directors may constitute such a governing authority. Indeed, corporations only exist in so far as "there is a *probability* that designated persons will act in such a way as to express the true meaning of the laws governing the group," and that group continues to exist even if there are widespread changes in specific personnel (108, emphasis in original).

This emphasis on the way economic power is converted into political influence does not deny that there may be a broad range of motives for contributing money to political parties. These motives may include interest in influencing government policy (Adamany 1972); personal involvement with an individual or group (Heard 1962); political access or an eagerness to solicit government privileges (Heard 1962; Thayer 1973); or even a sense of civic responsibility. In the final analysis, there really is no difference between selfish and unselfish motives for giving because both lead to a preference for a particular party or candidate.

The guiding thread of this study is the assumption that campaign finance contributions can be a reliable empirical indicator of the political preferences of people following their real material interests. The patterns in campaign contributions can be taken to reflect real differences and similarities in the perception of political interests between classes and class segments. At the same time, there may be some differences due to the crosscutting influences of personal preference, religion, and ethnicity.

This assumption concerning the nature of campaign finance contributions has been the basis for many recent studies of campaign finance—a growth area of political sociology in recent years (Clawson, Neustadtl and Beardon 1986; Burris 1987; Neustadtl and Clawson 1988; Allen and Broyles 1989; Clawson, Neustadtl and Scott 1992; Clawson, Neustadtl and Weller 1998), and in political science as well (Sabato 1989; Corrado 1992; Sorauf 1992; Gais 1996; Brown, Powell, and Wilcox 1995). This empirical research has focused upon contemporary political life, partly because of the availability of systematic campaign finance data provided by the Federal Election Commission (created by changes in campaign finance law following the Watergate scandal in the early 1970s).

A number of historical studies, however, have shown the importance of wealthy contributors to the political process, especially in presidential campaigns (e.g., Pollock 1926; Rochester 1936; Lundberg 1937; Overacker 1933, 1937, 1941, 1945, 1946; Heard 1962; Alexander 1971, 1976). With the same assumptions about the nature of campaign finance as more recent studies, these earlier studies have extensively documented the importance of contributions by business leaders (and to a lesser extent, organized labor) to presidential elections and provide a useful starting point for the analysis of New Deal campaign finance.

Most historical analyses of the relationship between business and political parties fail to systematically consider campaign finance data for 1936. This book seeks to rectify this oversight by using several data sources: all donations of more than $100, contributions from the Democratic Convention Book, and payments made by organized labor to various political organizations supporting Roosevelt's reelection. It draws on original analyses made by Louise Overacker, Michael Patrick Allen, and Ferdinand Lundberg for some of its evidence, as well as statistical data, autobiographies, and newspaper reports from the period. Although a $100 contribution might not seem particularly generous by today's standards, we have to remember that correcting for inflation, it would be equivalent to a donation of approximately $1,000 in 1995. At a time when average annual earnings were $1,184 per year and only 2.5 percent of American families had an annual income of $10,000 or more, a donation of $100 in 1936 was between 5 and 15 percent of total income for the great majority of American families (U.S. Bureau of the Census 1975:164, 300). A more detailed description of the data used in this book, along with a discussion of its limitations, can be found in the methodological appendix. Any understanding of campaign finance in the 1936 presidential election must take into account the larger social and political context, so it is necessary to outline the reasons for focusing on this particular election.

The Significance of the 1936 Presidential Election

There can be little doubt that the presidential election of 1936 represented a watershed in the history of the New Deal. The most important reform measures had been enacted into law between 1933 and 1936, including such landmark legislation as the Agricultural Adjustment Act 1933, the National Industrial Recovery Act 1933, the Securities Exchange Act 1934, the Banking Act 1935, the Social Security Act 1935, and the National Labor Relations Act 1935. The relief and welfare measures initiated by the federal government in the early New Deal earned Roosevelt enormous popular support among ordinary people and the slightly more guarded support of the business community.

By 1936, however, many business leaders discerned an antibusiness orientation to the Roosevelt Administration, which had not been totally apparent in 1932 (Leuchtenburg 1963:146–48; Wolfskill and Hudson 1969:154–59). This orientation apparently developed after the failure of the National Recovery Administration (NRA) in 1934 and the explosion of labor unrest in 1935. The Revenue Act of 1935 also "widened the split between Roosevelt and business leaders to an unbridgeable gulf" (Leff 1981:164). For many business leaders, their opposition to the ever-popular Roosevelt was not merely a symbolic gesture but reflected a genuine—if not passionate—desire to remove him from office.

During the campaign, Roosevelt fiercely attacked what he saw as a selfish and atavistic business community, intent on destroying the fabric of the New Deal's attempt to help the poor and marginalized (Leuchtenburg 1963:146–48; Wolfskill and Hudson 1969:154–59; Leff 1981:164; Badger 1989:98). In campaign speeches across the nation, he denounced the shortsighted and self-serving "economic royalists" in big business, banking, and Republican-owned newspapers who had changed the American economy into "privileged enterprise not free enterprise." This indicated that he was willing to use the power of the federal government to protect ordinary Americans against the "economic tyranny" of wealthy business leaders (Savage 1991:117–20). The antagonism toward anti–New Deal business leaders was increasingly framed in the rhetoric of class conflict. Although this may have resulted in a decline of campaign contributions from business, it increased support from organized labor, whose contributions steadily rose from more than $800,000 in 1936 to $1.3 million in 1944 (Overacker 1946:59).

The election is therefore significant because the Democratic and Republican parties "divided on issues in 1936 as they had at no previous time this century" (Leuchtenburg 1995:103). The parties clearly represented two opposing sets of assumptions regarding the role of government: a strong, interventionist welfare state versus a weak, free-market state, and these assumptions were increasingly framed in class terms. Roosevelt denounced the business community for feverishly trying to unravel the fabric of the New Deal, while the Republicans were equally vitriolic in their attacks on socialistic "big government" and the terrifying specter of government intrusion into private life (Leuchtenburg 1963:146–48, 1995:104; Wolfskill and Hudson 1969:154–59). Liberals and organized labor were clearly aligned with the Democratic Party, and at least the most visible and vociferous business leaders backed the Republicans.

In the election, Roosevelt defeated Republican Alfred M. Landon by a landslide (60.8 percent of the popular vote) and the Democrats won large majorities in the Senate (75-16) and the House (331-88). Furthermore, Roosevelt won 76 percent of lower-income voters (but only 42 percent of upper-income voters), 81 percent of unskilled laborers, 80 percent of labor union members, 84 percent of relief recipients, 86 percent of the Jewish vote, and up to 81 percent of the Catholic vote (Sachar 1992:460; Leuchtenburg 1995:153–56). According to most later analysts, in 1936 the Democrats consolidated the "New Deal coalition" despite unparalleled opposition from what many saw as a united business community. The result represented one of the most striking examples of critical realignment in this century, a seismic shift in electoral patterns that redefined the basis of political loyalties for a generation (Key 1955; Burnham 1970; Sundquist 1973; Brady 1988; Clubb, Flanigan, and Zingale 1990; Shafer 1991; Nardulli 1995). The election solidified the power of the new Democratic majority and made ordinary voters the focus of political transformation.

DETERMINING THE PARTY PREFERENCES OF BUSINESS

Although the general image of the 1936 election is one of a business community united behind the Republicans, several commentators have noted that some business leaders supported the Democrats, such as Sosthenes Behn of ITT, Sidney Weinberg of Goldman, Sachs, Amadeo P. Giannini of Bank of America, and New Orleans financier Rudolph Hecht (Schlesinger 1958:494; Leuchtenburg 1963:189–90; 1995:132). Other analysts have argued that specific business sectors—whether capital intensive, mass consumption, or Keynesian—supported the Democrats (Ferguson 1984, 1995; Friedlander 1987; Fraser 1989). To assess these various claims and determine which, if any, business leaders supported the Democrats, it is necessary to establish a baseline of Democratic donors within the business community.

To construct this baseline, I drew a random sample of 3,098 donors of more than $100 from the data set compiled by political scientist Louise Overacker (1937) from the official records submitted by both parties at the time of the election (see the methodological appendix for further details). In this sample, 32.8 percent of donors were Democrats and 67.2 percent were Republicans. Although this imbalance certainly suggests that well-to-do people favored the Republicans, it does not reveal anything of the party preferences of businessmen in 1936. To find out if any members of the business community were differentially favorable to the Democrats, I compared the sample of donors with the alphabetical list of officers and directors of corporations listed in *Poor's Register of Directors of the United States and Canada, 1936,* which lists people affiliated with businesses ranging in size from very small to very large in all business sectors. This analysis showed that only 31 percent of all large donors were listed in *Poor's*— which suggests that nearly 70 percent of them were small businessmen, professionals, or successful commercial farmers. More important, only 17 percent of the donors listed in *Poor's* gave to the Democrats. This figure is used as the Democratic baseline percentage throughout this book and is used to assess claims about differential support for the Democrats from various business sectors. That is, it is assumed for analytical purposes that 17 percent of the business leaders in any business sector are Democratic supporters, and that statistically significant percentages above that baseline percentage reveal an atypical Democratic preference.

In some instances I also looked at the party preferences of top business leaders in the very largest corporations, banks, and insurance companies. As an indicator of whether a person was a "top business leader," I determined which of the donors listed in *Poor's* were also affiliated with the largest 200 nonfinancial corporations, 30 commercial banks, 20 investment houses, or 20 insurance companies on a list of the top 270 companies for 1936. Allen (1991) compiled this list of companies based upon data collected by the Temporary National Economic Committee (TNEC) in the late 1930s.

There are several ways to present nominal data such as that presented and analyzed in this book (e.g., Reynolds 1984; Bohrnstedt and Knoke 1994), but preference is given to percentage differences in two-by-two tables using chi-square as the significance test for several reasons. First, this is as good as log linear analysis for my purposes because the magnitudes of campaign contributions are not being used, only the presence or absence of donations to each party, and because there is no ordering principle that would allow business sectors to be placed along a continuum (e.g., Kennedy 1992:1, 49). Second, there is reason to believe that useful chi-square values can be obtained with expected cell frequencies as low as one when the n is 20, without any correction for continuity (Camilli and Hopkins 1978, 1979; Camilli 1995). In addition, chi-square is equivalent in a two-by-two table to a test for the significance of differences between two independent proportions; that is, $x^2 = z^2$ (Ferguson 1981:211–13). Third, the percentage data in a two-by-two table allow us to report a correlational statistic and the effect sizes as well. Specifically, the Pearson r for dichotomous variables is equal to the percentage difference between the two cells in the top row of a two-by-two table (Rosenthal and Rubin 1982) and both the effect size phi (ϕ) and effect size lambda (λ) are also equal to the same percentage difference in a two-by-two table. That is, $r = \phi = \lambda$. Thus, chi-squares and Pearson rs will be reported for each analysis, with the understanding that the Pearson r is the same as the effect sizes phi and lambda in this instance.

In addition to looking at the overall percentage of directors in each business sector giving to either party, I also looked at those who were inside directors—members of the board of directors who were also officers of the company—and outside directors—usually officers and directors of other companies, financiers, bankers, corporate lawyers, or wealthy individual stockholders. This distinction is important for two reasons. First, it provides a way of establishing whether those directors who worked for a given company have a different pattern to their donations than those who are less directly involved with it. Second, it is important because some analysts think the inclusion of outside directors samples the economy in general, not the firm or industry under examination (Ferguson 1995:213).

There are two important general findings that help provide a proper context for the specific findings that are presented in later chapters. First, one of the most striking findings in the analysis of each business sector is how small a percentage of business people gave money to either party—a finding generally true for both inside and outside directors. This is also consistent with the findings of Allen (1991) for the 1930s, Heard (1962) for the 1950s, and Alexander (1971) and Domhoff (1972) for the 1960s. Second, virtually no business leaders gave to both political parties in 1936. The few who did usually gave to the Democrats after Roosevelt won the election. This means that the results on the individual level are clear cut in terms of party preference. In addition to comparing the party preferences of inside and outside directors in a wide range of business sectors, this book also analyzes business donors in terms of two very salient factors in American history, namely, region and religion, to explore the possibility that they are as important in shaping the party preferences of business leaders as they are in influencing other aspects of American politics. If it is found that the overrepresentation of Democratic business donors in a given business sector is due to regional or religious variables, then the apparent importance of business sectors in shaping party preferences is seriously undermined.

An Outline of What Is to Follow

Building on the approach outlined in the previous section, the following chapters use large financial donations to the 1936 presidential campaign to examine several general claims concerning the party preferences of different business and union leaders. In chapter 2, Overacker's claim that the bankers "deserted" the Democrats in 1936 is examined using a more rigorous methodology than she employed. Chapter 3 looks at the claim that Democrats were supported by mass-consumption industries (who benefited from the high level of consumer demand generated by Democratic relief and welfare policies). Chapter 4 examines the question of whether a capital-intensive, internationalist segment of the capitalist class dominated the Democratic Party from behind the scenes, despite appearances to the contrary. Chapter 5 presents a detailed analysis of the controversy surrounding contributions made to the Democrats via the convention book of 1936. In chapter 6, region and religion are examined in more depth through a detailed analysis of two key centers of Democratic electoral and financial support—New York City and the South. Chapter 7 looks at the role of organized labor, which, for the first time, played a significant role in American electoral politics.

The overall result of this analysis is that the business leaders who gave to the Democrats often differed from the great majority of business donors in terms of region and religion, and also tended to be from smaller companies. One of the few exceptions—the brewing industry—was unique in that it had been revived by the Democrats' lifting of Prohibition. In short, the biggest of "New Deal fat cats" did not underwrite the Democratic Party in 1936. Instead, most of the party's money came from business leaders on the fringes of the business community and from labor leaders. Specifically, the relatively few business leaders who gave to the Democrats tended to be Southerners, Jews, or Catholics. The party was, as William Mayer suggests, a "party of peripheral regions and disaffected minorities," (1996:98) a fact that was to have enormous consequences for the future development of the Democratic Party.

2

Deserters and Traitors: Did Business Desert The Democrats Between 1932 and 1936?

One of the most enduring claims concerning the financing of the 1936 Presidential election is that business leaders who had supported Roosevelt in 1932 deserted him in 1936. In particular, some New Deal historians have suggested that there was a sharp decline in support from bankers and brokers, an assertion based on evidence purporting to show that although in 1932, 24 percent of Democratic contributions of more than $1,000 came from bankers and brokers, less than 4 percent of such donations came from this source in 1936 (Schlesinger 1960:594; Leuchtenberg 1963:188, 1995:132).

The claim that many bankers deserted the Democrats between 1932 and 1936 is based on an analysis by Overacker (1937), a pioneer in the use of campaign finance data as an empirical indicator of the political preferences of business leaders. After examining the full range of contributing business sectors, Overacker showed the similarities and differences in business sources from which Democrats and Republicans obtained their funds. Primarily concerned with the influence of big business on electoral politics, her painstaking research on the 1930s contributed greatly to our understanding of the political preferences of various business leaders during the New Deal era.

Overacker's analysis of the economic interests of campaign contributors in 1936 showed that American business (particularly manufacturing industries) overwhelmingly favored the election of a Republican president, as it had in 1932 (1933:776–78; 1937:484–90). The initial focus of this chapter, however, is on

Overacker's most dramatic claim concerning campaign finance in 1936: that there was a "revolt of bankers and brokers from the Democratic Party" between 1932 and 1936 (1937:484). After examining the alleged flight of the bankers, I will investigate the broader issue of who deserted the Democratic Party in 1936, giving particular attention to the role of the Du Pont business network. In subsequent chapters, the following conclusion will set the stage for understanding the real business supporters of the New Deal: only those business leaders already alienated by the nomination of Roosevelt in 1932 deserted him in 1936.

THE REVOLT OF THE BANKERS FROM THE
DEMOCRATIC PARTY IN 1936

The hostility of many bankers and financiers toward the Roosevelt Administration is well documented (see, for example, Schlesinger 1960:501–12; Leuchtenburg 1963:150; Badger 1989:99), but Overacker goes further by suggesting that this hostility manifested itself in a dramatic shift in the campaign contributions of bankers from the Democrats to the Republicans in the 1936 presidential election, a revolt she labels as startling (1937:484).

The accuracy of Overacker's claim is called into question when its basis is identified as an incorrect inference from the differing percentage of large campaign contributions ($1,000 or more) by bankers in 1932 and 1936. She estimates that 24.2 percent of such Democratic contributions came from bankers in 1932, but dropped to 3.3 percent in 1936. Overacker concludes that bankers must have abandoned the Democrats. This difference, however, does not necessarily tell us anything if there were more $1,000–plus contributors in 1936 than in 1932, as is indeed the case: there were 280 Democratic donors who gave $1,000 or more in 1932 and 385 in 1936. To correct for this problem, I examined the 1936 contributions of the 40 Democratic and 64 Republican donors identified by Overacker as bankers in 1932.

To give this comparison a proper context, it is necessary to establish the general turnover rate for donors between 1928 and 1932, and then between 1932 and 1936. For the first comparison, Overacker claims there was a dramatic turnover in large contributions to the Democratic Party. Only 26 percent of those giving more than $1,000 in 1928 contributed in 1932, and only 44 percent of those who gave $25,000 or more contributed more than $1,000 in 1932. The turnover among Republicans was not so large, with less than 50 percent of those giving $1,000 or more in 1928 giving again in 1932. Of the group that gave $25,000 or more in 1928, 58 percent gave more than $1,000 in 1932 (1933:779–80).

For the 1932 to 1936 comparison, I conducted a new analysis that compared all 275 Democratic donors of $1,000 or more in 1932 with a representative sample of 275 comparable Republican donors from the larger number (522) of $1,000–plus Republican donors in 1932. To determine the degree of turnover from 1932 to 1936 for each party, a "repeat donor" was defined as any of the 275 Democrats or Republicans who gave $100 or more in 1936—thus increasing the possible percentage of repeat donors. Both parties had very high turnover rates (as defined by the percentage of nonrepeaters), although the Republican rate was slightly lower than that of the Democrats (see table 2.1); the difference between the two parties for the 1932/1936 comparison is not significant ($x = 1.21$, $p = .27$). Because the difference between the percentages in the top row of a two-by-two table is equal to the Pearson r for two dichotomous variables, we can also say the correlation between party and turnover rate for large donors is .05 for the 1932/1936 comparison.

The next step is to compare the Democratic donors whom Overacker identified as bankers with all other large donors to the Democratic Party in 1932 to find any differences in turnover rates.

TABLE 2.1

TURNOVER RATES IN CAMPAIGN FINANCE CONTRIBUTIONS
FOR REPUBLICAN AND DEMOCRATIC CONTRIBUTORS IN
PRESIDENTIAL ELECTIONS (1932–36)

	Democrats	Republicans
Repeaters	110 (40%)	135 (45%)
Nonrepeaters	162 (60%)	165 (55%)

Chi-square = 1.21; $p = 0.27$; Pearson $r = 0.05$

As seen in table 2.2, the difference is not statistically significant: the correlation between bankers and turnover rate is .06.

As table 2.3 reveals, Republican bankers were significantly more loyal than Democratic bankers in 1936—a fact that is interesting in itself, but does not establish that bankers "revolted" against the Democrats.

To look more specifically at the issue of revolt, I divided the nonrepeating bankers for both parties into two groups: those who gave nothing to either party in 1936 and those who switched parties. From this comparison we learn that seven prominent 1932 Democratic donors (Frank Alshul, Robert Goelet, Frank Phillips, Walter W. Price, F. H. Rawson, Roland Redmond, and Arthur Sachs) switched to the Republicans in 1936. By contrast, three 1932 Republican donors—Marshall Field, L.B. Manning, and George M. Moffett—switched to the Democrats. Thus, the Democrats had a net loss of only four bankers to the Republicans between 1932 and 1936. As table 2.4 demonstrates, the difference

TABLE 2.2

TURNOVER RATES IN CAMPAIGN FINANCE CONTRIBUTIONS FOR
DEMOCRATIC BANKERS AND OTHER DEMOCRATIC CONTRIBUTORS
IN PRESIDENTIAL ELECTIONS (1932–36)

	Democratic Bankers	Other Democratic Contributors
Repeaters	14 (35%)	96 (41%)
Non-repeaters	26 (65%)	139 (59%)

Chi-square = 4.88; p = 0.49; Pearson r = 0.06

TABLE 2.3

TURNOVER RATES IN CAMPAIGN FINANCE CONTRIBUTIONS OF
REPUBLICAN AND DEMOCRATIC BANKERS IN PRESIDENTIAL
ELECTIONS (1932–36)

	Democratic Bankers	Republican Bankers
Repeaters	14 (35%)	39 (63%)
Non-repeaters	26 (65%)	23 (37%)

Chi square = 7.58; p = 0.006; Pearson r = 0.28

TABLE 2.4

REPUBLICAN AND DEMOCRATIC BANKERS WHO MADE NO DONATIONS OR
SWITCHED PARTIES (1932–36)

	Democratic Bankers	Republican Bankers
Switching Parties	7 (27%)	3 (13%)
Non-Donation	19 (73%)	20 (87%)

Chi-square $= 1.45$; $p = 0.23$; Pearson $r = 0.14$

between Republicans and Democrats switching parties is not statistically significant.

There is one final point to make before drawing any conclusions about contributions from bankers. The single largest donor to the Democrats in 1932, John J. Raskob, was incorrectly counted by Overacker as a banker. Although he sat on the boards of several small banks, he began his career in 1902 as the personal secretary of Pierre S. Du Pont. By 1928, Raskob was the treasurer of E. I. Du Pont de Nemours Corporation and treasurer and chairman of the finance committee of General Motors. He resigned from the GM post in 1928 in order to assume control of the Democratic National Committee (Burk 1990:8), but remained an important part of the Du Pont family and business circles.

Although Overacker was somewhat hesitant about including Raskob in her list of bankers—noting he was primarily a Du Pont executive—her caution has been overlooked by those who have made generalizations from her overall analysis. One-third of the total contributions from bankers in 1932 came from Raskob, but they were not contributions in the usual sense. They were primarily canceled debts totaling $100,000—originally given to the 1928 presidential campaign of his friend Al Smith (Overacker 1933:777). In 1932, Raskob was not at all enthusiastic about Roosevelt's bid for the presidency. Excluding Raskob, only 17 percent of $1,000–plus Democratic contributions came from the bankers in 1932 as opposed to 20.5 percent for Republicans.

There is little evidence to support the idea of a bankers' revolt from the Democrats in 1936, and if high turnover rates are seen as a revolt, it should be noted that it was not restricted to bankers or even Democrats and that it occurred in 1928–32 as well. Add to this the fact that Democrats had a net loss of only four bankers to the Republicans, and the anecdotal nature of the claim about the revolt of the bankers becomes even more apparent.

WHO DID DESERT THE DEMOCRATS IN 1936?

Eliminating the theory of a bankers' revolt in 1936 still leaves the question of whether there were any desertions from the Democratic Party. The answer can be found in the actions of some members of the Du Pont business empire who were allied with dissident conservative Democrats. Overacker noted that less than one-third of those who gave $1,000 or more in 1932 gave to the Democrats in 1936, and that many prominent contributors gave to the Republicans (including Edward S. Harkness, William Randolph Hearst, and William K. Vanderbilt) (1937:494)—but the most prominent of these was Pierre S. Du Pont.

Of all the very wealthy families in the United States in the 1930s, few were as rich as the Du Ponts. The family is of French descent (emigrating to the United States in 1800), and the foundation of the family fortune was laid by Pierre S. Du Pont, who ensured that subsequent to World War I, the E. I. Du Pont de Nemours chemical company would grow into one of the most powerful corporations in the world (Allen 1987:42–51). By 1936, it was worth nearly $720 million, and even at the height of the depression company profits climbed from $26 million in 1932 to over $90 million in 1936 (Zilg 1974:345).

The company was only one part of an extensive corporate network owned or controlled by the Du Ponts through substantial minority stockholdings. The key company in the network was Christiana Securities—a family holding company that owned about 25 percent of voting stock in E. I. Du Pont de Nemours, which in turn had the same proportionate interest in General Motors Corporation (U.S. National Resources Committee 1939:313). The Du Ponts and their representatives dominated the management of both GM and E. I. Du Pont de Nemours. Furthermore, the Du Ponts controlled about 20 percent of voting stock in United States Rubber Company through yet another holding company called Rubber Securities. They also owned the National Bank of Detroit, which had five General Motors officials on its board of directors. By 1938, the three industrial giants and one bank at the center of the Du Pont empire had assets of approximately $2.6 billion. This did not include the profits generated from other large companies in the Du Pont network such as Wilmington Trust Company, Equitable Trust Company, Continental American Life Insurance, Delaware Trust Company, North American Aviation, Remington Arms Company, and New York Air Brake Company.

Without question, the most lucrative part of the network was General Motors Corporation, which had assets of $1.5 billion in 1936. The Du Ponts received 20–30 percent of their total income from General Motors, earning annual profits for the family of up to $225 million. In 1936, 350 officers and directors of General Motors were paid $10 million in salaries and bonuses. In contrast, the average General Motors factory worker earned a yearly wage of $900—well below the $1,600 the federal government regarded as the minimum income with which a family of four could live decently (Zilg 1974:330).

Most Du Ponts and their top-level employees were Republicans until the late 1920s. They were conservative and elitist to the core, with a strong belief that senior business executives who had survived and prospered in the fiercely competitive environment of the free market were best suited to lead the nation. Demagogic politicians, they argued, were only concerned with satisfying the selfish demands of their constituents. Ultimately, the Du Ponts' aversion to government intervention, their support of extreme right-wing political organizations, and their hatred of Franklin D. Roosevelt was based on a distrust of popular democracy and on their belief that only enlightened corporate stewardship (under Du Pont auspices) could save America (Wolfskill 1962: Burk 1990).

The Du Ponts became more directly involved in politics and turned toward the Democratic Party because of their growing hostility toward Prohibition, as several accounts explain (e.g., Zilg 1974:236–42; Burk 1990:81–85), but there is still disagreement as to why they became such staunch foes of the eighteenth amendment. One theory is that their ratio of wealth to income was well below average, making them peculiarly susceptible to changes in taxation. The Du Pont business empire therefore wholeheartedly embraced the repeal of Prohibition in order to allow the government to tax liquor and thereby lower, or even abolish, income tax. This objective was concealed by public claims that Prohibition wasted enormous tax revenues both in lost liquor taxes and in expenditures made enforcing its laws.

Another theory (held by many scholars) maintains that the Du Ponts opposed Prohibition because it represented a significant increase in federal power—power that could be used to promote social values and political regulations hostile to their interests (e.g., Kerr 1985:277; Blocker 1989:121). In their view, not only was the government attempting to regulate personal habits and individual behavior, it had also completely failed to enforce restrictions on the manufacture, sale, transport, and importation of alcohol. This all caused the Du Ponts some distress because the continuing resentment against Prohibition was undermining respect for the rule of law (Kyvig 1979:88; Rumbarger 1989:192). They believed the activist, reformist state should be stopped and replaced by a neutral and compliant state—willing and able to act on behalf of capital (Kyvig 1985:15; Blocker 1989:121). As John Rumbarger has argued, the political goal of Prohibition's corporate opponents was not repeal. "Rather, it was the preservation of capitalists' ability to intervene directly through the state into any such aspects of the nation's social life that appeared threatening to corporate business" (1989:192).Whatever motives propelled the Du Pont family into action, they assumed a leadership role in 1926 with the major organization seeking repeal, the Association Against the Prohibition Amendment (AAPA), founded in 1918. With the Republican Party irretrievably committed to Prohibition, the anti-Prohibitionists in the Du Pont network gravitated toward the Democrats for the realization of their political objectives. The Democrats were largely ambivalent about Prohibition and therefore likely to be converted to the anti-Prohibitionists' ultimate objective: repeal of the Eighteenth Amendment.

Raskob, who as assistant to Pierre Du Pont previously had shown little interest in politics, forged ties to the Democrats in early 1927 through his developing friendship with presidential hopeful Alfred E. Smith. The two men shared a common Catholic faith, a love of New York City, and a "rags-to-riches" background (Rosen 1977:27; Burk 1990:41). More important for the Du Ponts, not only was Smith opposed to Prohibition, but he was also fiscally conservative, and reluctant to let government intervene in the economy. When Smith appointed Raskob chairman of the Democratic Party (against the advice of liberal Democrats), the Du Ponts recognized an opportunity to turn the party away from its liberal leanings and create a "conservative instrument in national affairs" (Rosen 1977:28).

Despite his large donation of $540,000 in direct contributions, loans, and promissory notes, Raskob proved to be a major political liability in Smith's unsuccessful bid for the presidency in 1928. Raskob alienated many Southerners by his failure to understand agricultural policy, he further inflamed anti-Catholic sentiments, and he projected a pro-business image for the Democrats, despite his inability to attract much business support (Burk 1990:52–53). Nevertheless, the campaign marked the beginning of the Du Ponts' involvement in the financial fortunes of the Democratic Party. The business community as a whole, however, was satisfied with Republican prosperity and did not see Prohibition as a major issue. Raskob and Pierre Du Pont even had problems raising money among other members of the Du Pont circle, such as Irénée and Lammot Du Pont, who continued to give to the Republicans.

Smith's defeat in 1928 did not diminish Raskob's influence in the Democratic National Committee headquarters. With the approval and support of Pierre S. Du Pont, Raskob attempted to use his position as party chairman to restructure the party—creating a permanent, centralized party organization to prepare for future elections. Much of the financing for this effort came from Raskob himself. By the end of 1930, he had contributed approximately $875,000 more to the Democratic Party (around $30,000 per month), with most of it going to his good friend Jouett Shouse's salary as DNC executive committee chairman (Burk 1990:62–63). In the mid-term election of 1930, the Democrats gained fifty-three House seats and eight Senate seats—probably as a result of the depression. Pierre S. Du Pont interpreted this success as evidence that the Democrats were the party of repeal.

In October 1931, Raskob established a little-known "Victory Fund" in an effort to increase business influence within the party. By January 1932, it had raised $500,000—mainly from ex-Smith supporters such as William F. Kenny, Bernard Baruch, Herbert Lehman, Pierre S. Du Pont, and John J. Raskob himself (Burk 1990:89–90). But after the Democratic convention in July 1932, Roosevelt replaced Raskob with James A. Farley as chairman of the Democratic National Committee. It was the beginning of the end for Du Pont influence in the party.

Despite their serious misgivings about the candidacy of Franklin D. Roosevelt, the Du Pont circle continued to support the Democrats in the 1932 election. Before the convention they had preferred, and had campaigned for, a more conservative Democrat in line with their views. Nevertheless, Roosevelt's victory and initial reforms of the New Deal won support from the Du Pont circle. They were pleased with the administration's efforts to repeal Prohibition and with its creation of the National Recovery Administration, even though its formation marked the beginning of conflict over whether the agency would be a vehicle of government planning or, as the Du Ponts desired, industrial self-government (Burk 1990:112–13).

Expanded government intervention in economic management, especially with regard to unionization, only magnified the Du Ponts' apprehension and sense of foreboding about Roosevelt's intentions. Their support for the Democrats had always been based on pragmatic political calculation, so the unexpected leftward drift of the Roosevelt Administration elicited increasingly bitter and vitriolic criticism from the Du Ponts (Burk 1990:130–32). By mid-May 1934, Pierre S. Du Pont had stopped all payments that would have reduced the Democratic Party's debts. When he and his family formed the American Liberty League in August 1934, it heralded the beginning of outright Du Pont-Raskob opposition to Roosevelt.

It is clear, therefore, that the most significant desertion from the Democratic Party in 1936 was by the Du Pont group, including Raskob, who only joined the party in 1928 temporarily, over the Prohibition issue. By September 1936, the Du Ponts had given $385,000 to the Republican Party, including donations of $105,000 from Lammot Du Pont, $100,000 from Irénée Du Pont, and $85,000 from Pierre (Burk 1990:244). A disillusioned Raskob did not make any campaign contributions to the major parties. At the same time, the Du Ponts increased their support of the anti-

Roosevelt American Liberty League. In 1935, 30 percent of League funds came from the Du Pont family, and in 1936 they provided 25 percent (Wolfskill 1962:63). In addition to this support, the Du Pont business network gave substantial sums of money to other right-wing groups such as the Crusaders, the Sentinels of the Republic, the American Taxpayers League, the Farmers Independence League, the Economists National Committee, and the Southern Committee to Uphold the Constitution (Wolfskill 1962:228–42; Zilg 1974:314–26). Large financial capitalists supplied nearly 90 percent of the funding for anti–New Deal and antiradical groups, with the Du Ponts providing $350,000 of the $1 million given to such organizations. Other major contributions came from the Pitcairn, Morgan, Rockefeller, and Hutton groups (Almond 1998:225).

The Du Ponts also funded the efforts of dissident Democrats to unseat Roosevelt. These old line, professional politicians (many of whom had supported Woodrow Wilson) included: the chief counsel of the House of Morgan and 1924 Democratic presidential candidate John W. Davis; former New York governor and 1928 Democratic presidential candidate, Alfred E. Smith; former conservative Democratic governor of Maryland, Albert Richie; former Democratic governor of Massachusetts, Joseph E. Ely; and former Wilson Secretary of War, Newton D. Baker. They had reluctantly supported the Democrats in 1932, but in 1936 openly opposed Roosevelt's reelection (Gosnell 1952:144; Schlesinger 1960:517–19; Leuchtenburg 1963:177–79). Many of them believed that Roosevelt "had jettisoned virtues like character, thrift, and self-reliance, had forsaken goals like the equality of opportunity to compete for a new emphasis on security and social rights and had given himself over to a brazen cadre of planners" (Leuchtenburg 1963:177). In early August 1936, "forty prominent ex-New Deal Democrats" came together to organize the National Jefferson Democrats to oppose Roosevelt's reelection. They received much of their funding from Liberty Leaguers such as Ernest T. Weir, owner of Weirton Steel; Alfred P. Sloan, president of General Motors; and of course, Pierre S. Du Pont and John J. Raskob, directors of General Motors (Wolfskill 1962:196–98).

Wolfskill (1962:192–98) provides the names of ten National Jefferson Democrats, including such political nonbusiness notables as Bainbridge Colby, Henry Breckinridge, and Joseph W. Bailey Jr. A check of *Poor's Register of Directors,* 1936 reveals that only John Henry Kirby, a Texas lumberman, was a corporate director, and with the sole exception of Colby, who gave $2,500 to the Democrats in 1932, none of the ten made a campaign contribution to either party in 1932 or 1936. Furthermore, the board of directors and the national executive committee of the American Liberty League (twenty-five people) were checked against *Who's Who in America,* 1936–37 to find out how many members identified themselves as Democrats. Of the eight self-identified Democrats, none made campaign contributions in 1932. In 1936, there were only two contributors from the board: Robert Lund gave $1,500 to the Republicans in October 1936 and Raoul E. Desvernine gave $1,500 to the Democrats in May 1935.

Clearly, the main Democratic deserters in 1936 were members of the Du Pont business network, together with a group of conservative, nonbusiness Democrats whose attachment to the party was in question as early as 1932. Given the empirical evidence presented in this chapter, it is unlikely that many major business leaders, bankers or nonbankers, deserted the Democrats in 1936. In fact, most prominent business leaders were Republicans in 1932 and 1936, with manufacturers providing 26.3 percent of contributions of more than $1,000 in 1932 and 29.6 percent in 1936.

Who did support the Democrats in 1936? The answer to this question unfolds gradually over the remainder of the book as several rival theoretical claims are measured against the systematic empirical data compiled by Overacker. Despite my specific criticism of her claim about "desertion" by bankers, the overall thrust of my findings is that she is more accurate about the sources of party campaign funds than many later theorists.

useful to take a more detailed look at who they were, beginning with the powerful Straus family (owners of R. H. Macy), who were in many ways emblematic of Jewish presence in the industry.

The Straus family comprised long-standing Democrats who eventually forged relatively close ties to the Roosevelt Administration. The R. H. Macy department store was originally purchased by Isidor Straus in 1874 from Rowland Hussey Macy (a Quaker whaler turned shopkeeper) (Harris 1977:39). After Isidor and his wife, Ida Blum, perished in the *Titanic* disaster of 1912, control of R. H. Macy fell to their sons Percy, Jesse Isidor, and Herbert Nathan. By that time the family lineage in political life was firmly established because their uncles Oscar and Nathan were well known in liberal and progressive circles. Oscar Straus was U.S. ambassador to Turkey for twenty years and earned such a high reputation for public service that Republican president Theodore Roosevelt appointed him secretary of commerce and labor in December 1906. He was the first Jew ever to serve on the Cabinet. Nathan Straus (a former New York City Park Commissioner who resigned in 1914) devoted himself to charity and gave away two-thirds of his fortune by the time of his death in 1931 (Harris 1977:44–49). By 1936, Percy, Jack Isidor, and Ralph I. Straus (all Democratic contributors) were the only family members still on the board of R. H. Macy (39).

The family's ties to the Democratic Party did not end there. Jesse Isidor Straus was an ardent and active conservative Democrat who was appointed by Governor Roosevelt in 1931 to head New York State's Temporary Emergency Relief Administration, where he hired future New Dealer Harry Hopkins. In early 1936, he organized the Roosevelt Business and Professional League and urged businessmen throughout the country to support FDR. He was appointed U.S. ambassador to France by Roosevelt in 1933 and served in that capacity until his death in October 1936 (*New York Times* 1936a).

Also a strong Democratic supporter and vice chairman of the Democratic National Finance Committee in 1928 was the austere Percy Straus who, before entering Harvard in 1893, was educated at Sach's School in New York along with such Jewish luminaries of finance and journalism as Herbert Lehman, Henry Morgenthau, Mortimer Schiff, and Walter Lippman. Although he continued to support Roosevelt throughout the 1930s, Percy became anxious about government intervention in economic affairs and began to criticize the New Deal, particularly after the Social Security Act and the National Labor Relations Act became laws in 1935 (*New York Times* 1944). The remaining Straus contributors who were also directors of R. H. Macy were Jack Isidor (the future head of the company, and son of Jesse Isidor) and Percy's son Ralph Isidor. A family cousin, Hugh Grant Straus (son of philanthropist Nathan Straus and a director of Federated Department Stores) also contributed to the Democrats.

The Strauses were not the only prominent American Jews from the department store industry supporting the Democrats. The ebullient Bernard F. Gimbel (founder of Gimbel Brothers and owner of Saks Fifth Avenue) was an influential figure in New York City politics, where he was (as his obituary so cryptically put it) an "advisor on major municipal improvements" (*New York Times* 1966). Gimbel was also well connected to the national Democratic leadership, having established close friendships with James A. Farley (Roosevelt's Postmaster General and campaign manager in 1936); Bernard Baruch, the well-known Democratic financier; and Jack I. Straus, the future head of R. H. Macy. Another important Democratic contributor was Ukrainian immigrant Albert M. Greenfield, who owned Lit Brothers and City Stores and developed a reputation for toughness unparalleled in the industry (Harris 1977:83–90). Throughout the 1920s, Greenfield was a committed Republican and had seconded Herbert Hoover's nomination for the presidency in 1928. He switched to Roosevelt in 1932, however, and quickly became one of the most powerful Democrats in Pennsylvania, helping to raise money for the party in every presidential election until he died in 1967 (*New York Times* 1967).

The two remaining Jewish Democratic contributors from the department store industry were John J. Turteltaub and Paul M. Mazur. Turteltaub was executive vice president of Greenfield's real estate company in New York City and was also a director of two other Greenfield corporations—City Stores and Bankers Securities Company (*New York Times* 1962). Mazur, a prominent Democratic fund raiser, was a partner with Lehman Brothers and also sat on the boards of Federated Department Stores and Allied Stores.

In the retail industry, there were only two non-Jewish contributors to the Democrats—George H. Johnson and Marshall Field—and their contributions are consistent with this study's emphasis on religion. As a prominent member of the Greenfield empire, George H. Johnson became president of Lit Brothers in 1933 and was later "drawn into the diversified business organizations developed by Albert M. Greenfield" (*New York Times* 1959). Marshall Field (an English-educated, New York millionaire with financial interests in railroads as well as in retail) was atypical of most business leaders of the time in that he was Roman Catholic.

There are two significant omissions from this list of Jewish Democratic contributors from the retail industry. Lincoln Filene and Louis Edward Kirstein were directors of Federated Department Stores, which owned majority stock in Filene Brothers, Abraham and Straus, F. and R. Lazarus, and Bloomingdales. In 1936, both men gave money to the Progressive Party rather than the Democrats, and both were steeped in the progressive politics then typical of Filene Brothers. Under the guidance of Lincoln's older brother, Edward A. Filene, and his lawyer, Louis D. Brandeis, the company had created the Filene Cooperative Association to administer medical services, eating facilities, insurance funds, and other welfare benefits to Filene employees (Harris 1977:10–35). Kirstein played an important role on the National Recovery Administration's Industrial Advisory Board, settling a number of disputes in the clothing and millinery industries (*New York Times* 1942), and his Twentieth Century Fund conducted a study largely supportive of the Wagner Act. Though not included in the data, Filene and Kirstein were nonetheless important supporters of New Deal reform.

Tobacco Industry

The tobacco industry also had a relatively high percentage of Democratic contributors (42 percent). Here I found yet another nonindustrial sector variable was responsible for its Democratic preference—namely region. During the 1930s, tobacco was the second largest industry in the South and accounted for more than

three-quarters of the nation's production of cigarettes and cigars
(Martin 1941:161). The industry was especially important in the
economies of North Carolina and Virginia, where the tobacco was
grown and processed. The cigarette industry was concentrated in
Richmond, Durham, and Winston-Salem, while cigar manufacturing took place mainly in Tampa, New Orleans, and Jacksonville
(163).

To study the tobacco industry, I took a stratified sample of
southern companies on the basis of size, according to the company's total worth in December 1936. This was matched with the
same number of northern companies (equivalent in product line
and number of employees) in order to provide regional compari-
sons. As table 3.4 shows, there was a north-south split in terms of
political affiliation: the southern tobacco companies had more
people contributing to the Democratic Party, while the northern
firms were firmly in the Republican camp.

As table 3.5 demonstrates, southern directors gave to the Democrats while the northern directors gave to the Republicans. The

TABLE 3.4

1936 CAMPAIGN CONTRIBUTIONS OF $100 OR MORE BY OFFICERS
AND DIRECTORS IN SELECTED NORTHERN AND SOUTHERN FIRMS
IN THE TOBACCO INDUSTRY

Company	Number of Directors/Officers	Number/Percent of Contributors	Number Republican	Democrat
North				
Liggert & Meyers	18	3 (17%)	3	—
General Cigar	10	3 (30%)	2	1
Consolidated Cigar	13	3 (23%)	3	—
Bayuk Cigars	13	2 (15%)	2	—
Total	54	11 (20%)	10 (90%)	1 (10%)
South				
R. J. Reynolds	12	8 (67%)	1	7
Phillip Morris	14	—	—	—
Universal Leaf	12	1 (8%)	1	—
Axton-Fisher	8	6 (75%)	1	5
Total	46	15 (33%)	3 (20%)	12 (80%)

TABLE 3.5

1936 PARTY CONTRIBUTIONS BY OFFICERS AND DIRECTORS IN THE
TOBACCO INDUSTRY (BY REGION)

	South	North
Democrats	80%	9%
Republicans	20%	91%
Total	100% (15)	100% (11)

Note: Number in parentheses shows total number of individuals.

$x^2 = 12.76; p = 0.0004; r = 0.71$

evidence presented seems to indicate that region, rather than
business sector, explains campaign contributions in this industry.

Brewing Industry

During the New Deal, leaders in the brewing industry contributed
differentially to the Democrats. As table 3.1 indicated, however, a
majority of those directors who made contributions were supporters of the Republicans. Furthermore, as table 3.6 makes clear, the
Republican preference was even sharper among the ten largest
brewing companies, where 25 percent of all officers and directors

TABLE 3.6

1936 CAMPAIGN CONTRIBUTIONS OF $100 OR MORE BY OFFICERS AND
DIRECTORS IN THE TEN LARGEST BREWING COMPANIES

Company	Number of Directors/Officers	Number/Percent of Contributors	Number Republican	Number Democrat
Standard Brands	24	7 (29%)	7	—
Schenley Distillers	13	5 (38%)	1	4
National Distillers	20	9 (45%)	5	4
Anheuser-Busch Inc.	18	8 (44%)	6	2
Froedtert Grain & Malting	9	2 (22%)	1	1
Continental Gin	26	0 (0%)	—	—
Pittsburgh Brewing	10	1 (10%)	1	—
Oldetyme Distillers	7	3 (43%)	1	2
Duquesne Brewing	7	—	—	—
Brown Foreman Distillery	7	1 (14%)	—	1
Total	141	36 (25%)	22 (61%)	14 (39%)

contributed to one of the two major parties (specifically, twenty-two contributed to the Republicans and only fourteen to the Democrats, a 61 to 39 percent difference). On the other hand, among the smaller brewing companies (eighteen companies with a value under $5 million), only 9.5 percent of officers and directors contributed—ten giving to the Democrats and five to the Republicans (67 to 33 percent). Overall, these findings demonstrate a very high level of financial support for the Democrats, considerably more than the 17 percent baseline percentage. Among all inside directors of the brewing industry there is an overwhelming preference for the Democrats (87 to 13 percent) and among directors of smaller companies there is a strong Democratic preference (67 to 33 percent), as already reported. What factor can account for this strong Democratic showing?

The crucial factor was that the Democratic Party ended Prohibition, thus reviving the industry. As Overacker observed, "liquor paid its debt of gratitude to the Democratic Party" by contributing en masse to Roosevelt's reelection campaign in 1936, giving 5.7 percent of the party's $1,000—plus contributions (1937:487). Inside directors in particular may have been especially grateful to the Democrats given that their primary material interests were more closely tied to the fate of liquor production than those of outside directors. Moreover, beer makers (the vast majority of whom were smaller companies producing primarily for local markets) were also grateful to Roosevelt because they had suffered disproportionately during Prohibition for two reasons. First, because of beer's bulk in relation to alcohol content, its production, transportation, and sale were the least profitable of any alcoholic beverage. Second, the depression deeply affected the income of its predominantly working-class consumers (Blocker 1989:119–20).

Food and Beverage Industry

For the purposes of this study, the food and beverage industry included the largest firms in baking, beverages, biscuits, canning, confectionery, and dairy together with a few miscellaneous companies. These firms represented approximately 10–15 percent of all firms listed in this industry. As table 3.7 shows, the industry as

TABLE 3.7

1936 CAMPAIGN CONTRIBUTIONS OF $100 OR MORE BY OFFICERS AND
DIRECTORS IN THE TEN LARGEST FOOD AND BEVERAGE COMPANIES

Company	Number of Directors/Officers	Number/Percent of Contributors	Number Republican	Democrat
Continental Baking (Baking)	18	6 (34%)	6	—
Coca-Cola (Beverage)	39	6 (15%)	—	6
National Biscuit (Biscuits)	25	10 (40%)	10	—
California Packing (Canning)	25	2 (8%)	2	—
Libby, McNeill & Libby (Canning)	16	2 (12%)	2	—
Wm. Wrigley Jr. (Confectionery)	13	4 (31%)	4	—
Borden Company (Dairy)	23	4 (17%)	4	—
United Fruit (Fruit Processing)	24	6 (25%)	4	2
Quaker Oats (Cereal)	22	14 (64%)	14	—
Corn Products Refining (Syrup & Starch)	18	9 (50%)	8	1
Total	223	63 (28%)	54 (86%)	9 (14%)

a whole was overwhelmingly Republican in its campaign contributions and among both inside directors (81 percent) and outside directors (92 percent).

The only firm to indicate strong Democratic sympathy was the Coca-Cola Company. In 1936, the Atlanta-based corporation was a medium-sized southern beverage operation—not the multinational giant it is today. In fact, its regional location might explain the campaign contributions of its board of directors better than any other variable. Of the six officers and directors who contributed, I found detailed biographical information about three—Samuel F. Boykin, Harold Hirsch, and Desales Harrison—and all three were Southerners.

Having demonstrated that the Democratic campaign contributions by leaders of the department store, tobacco, food and beverage, and brewing industries are primarily due to region and religion, I now turn to the only mass-consumption sectors that showed a decidedly Republican preference: the household electrical equipment industry and chain stores and mail order houses.

Household Electrical Equipment Industry

The electrical equipment industry produces such goods as refrigerators, vacuum cleaners, toasters, and cooking stoves. Because the sale of these items is almost entirely dependent on the level of consumer demand, it is reasonable to infer that these firms would be interested in increasing consumers' purchasing power and would be inclined to support the policies and programs of the Democratic Party. As table 3.8 demonstrates, however, the largest firms in this industry gave little evidence of Democratic support.

Virtually all the contributors in this industry gave to the Republicans. All inside directors and the vast majority of outside directors were Republican (83 percent). The solitary Democrat among the major companies was Earl Bailie, an outside director with Maytag Corporation who gave to the Democrats and was a non-Jewish partner in the German-Jewish investment bank of J. W. Seligman and Co.

Chain Stores and Mail Order Houses

By the mid-1930s, chain stores were beginning to standardize many of the routine purchases made by ordinary Americans and

TABLE 3.8

1936 CAMPAIGN CONTRIBUTIONS OF $100 OR MORE BY OFFICERS AND DIRECTORS IN MAJOR HOUSEHOLD ELECTRICAL EQUIPMENT COMPANIES

Company	Number of Directors/Officers	Number/Percent of Contributors	Number Republican	Democrat
Singer	7	1 (14%)	1	—
Nash-Kelvinator	19	3 (16%)	3	—
Servel	18	2 (11%)	2	—
Landers, Frary & Clark	22	—	—	—
Perfection Stove	15	5 (33%)	5	—
Maytag	9	2 (22%)	1	1
Total	90	13 (14%)	12 (92%)	1 (8%)

both their managerial structures and their product lines were becoming more rationalized and centralized (Cohen 1990:106).
These stores maintained the appearance of the local independent, however, and provided personal service (unlike the chain
store giants of today). In the major cities, such stores grew rapidly
during the interwar years, which pressured the mail-order houses
to open stores. In 1925, Sears Roebuck opened its first store in
Chicago and by the end of the decade had 324 nationwide; Mont-
gomery Ward entered the market with its first store in 1929
(Cohen 1990:107).

As table 3.9 demonstrates, the chain stores and mail order
houses contributed to the Republican campaign in 1936. This is
further supported by Overacker's conclusion that these segments
of the retail industry were Republican in 1936 (1937:488), leaving
none for the Democratic camp. The sole Democratic contributor
was Sidney Weinberg, a New York investment banker with Goldman, Sachs who sat on the board of Sears Roebuck. Weinberg
joined Goldman, Sachs in 1907 and became a partner twenty

TABLE 3.9

1936 CAMPAIGN CONTRIBUTIONS OF $100 OR MORE BY OFFICERS AND
DIRECTORS IN MAJOR CHAIN STORES AND MAIL ORDER HOUSES

Company	Number of Directors/Officers	Number/Percent of Contributors	Number Republicans	Democrat
Safeway Stores (Chain Store)	5	1 (20%)	1	—
S. S. Kresge (Chain Store)	12	7 (58%)	7	—
Great Atlantic & Pacific Tea Co. of America (Chain Store)	13	—	—	—
J. C. Penney (Chain Store)	15	3 (20%)	3	—
S. H. Kress (Chain Store)	14	1 (7%)	1	—
Montgomery Ward (Mail Order)	17	6 (35%)	6	—
Sears Roebuck (Mail Order)	22	2 (9%)	1	1
Total	98	20 (20%)	19 (95%)	1 (5%)

years later. He was on numerous corporate boards and worked as assistant treasurer of the Democratic National Committee in both 1932 and 1936.

KEYNESIAN ELITE

As a final probe into the mass-consumptionist thesis, I looked at the campaign contributions of nineteen firms named by Peter Friedlander (1987) as part of a "Keynesian elite." Rooted in the mass-consumption sector and committed to market expansion, government intervention, and regulatory reform, Friedlander claims the Keynesian elite saw the Democratic Party as the most appropriate political vehicle to achieve its objectives. As table 3.10 demonstrates, a significant majority of contributors gave to the Republicans, but this still left a large number of Democrats when compared to the 17 percent baseline percentage. Because of these results, I delved deeper into the religious backgrounds of these individuals via standard biographical sources.

This analysis showed that the sizable minority of support for Democrats within the Keynesian elite is best explained by religious affiliation. Among the sixty members of the elite, 67 percent of eighteen Jewish donors gave to the Democrats while 80 percent of forty-two non-Jewish donors gave to the Republicans. Such large religious differences would not exist if business considerations exclusively determined the party preferences of leaders in mass-consumption industries.

EXPLAINING THE DIFFERENCE BETWEEN INSIDE AND OUTSIDE DIRECTORS

At the outset, I referred to a split between inside and outside directors in terms of their Democratic preferences. Among inside directors, 34 percent gave to the Democrats compared to 18 percent of outside directors. The split can be explained in terms of regional and religious factors. Regarding inside directors of mass-consumption industries, twenty Democratic donors (of the thirty-two on whom biographical information could be found) were cat-

TABLE 3.10

1936 CAMPAIGN CONTRIBUTIONS OF $100 OR MORE BY OFFICERS
AND DIRECTORS OF COMPANIES CONSIDERED PART OF THE
KEYNESIAN ELITE

Company	Percent of Contributors	Number Contributing to Republicans	Democrats	Number of Officers/Directors
Goldman, Sachs	50%	2	1	6
Lehman Brothers	44%	3	1	9
Bank of America	5%	1	0	22
Bowery Savings Bank	29%	7	0	24
Curtis Publishing	8%	0	1	13
R. H. Macy	45%	2	3	11
Federated Dept. Stores*	56%	2	4	11
City Stores	23%	0	3	13
Lit Brothers	14%	0	2	14
F. W. Woolworth	11%	3	0	26
Marshall Field	23%	3	1	17
Dennison	0	0	0	9
Endicott Johnson	0	0	0	11
United Fruit	25%	4	2	24
American Tobacco	12%	1	1	17
IBM	22%	3	1	18
General Foods	38%	7	3	26
Eastman Kodak	0	0	0	24
Chrysler Corp.	50%	8	1	18
Total	22%	46 (66%)	24 (34%)	313

*Lincoln Filene and L. E. Kirstein of Federated Dept. Stores Co. gave to the Progressives
but are included among the Democrats for this table.

egorized as follows: ten were Southerners, nine were Jewish, and
one was Catholic. Of the remaining twelve Democratic inside directors, nine were from the brewing industry. Only seven of sixty-
three Republicans on whom biographical information could be
found were southern, Jewish, or Catholic.

CONCLUSION

As this chapter has shown, there is no evidence that mass-consumption industries were differentially Democratic for economic
reasons. When region and religion were controlled, the percent-

age of Democrats in the seven mass-consumption industries was no greater than the baseline percentage. The one industry where region and religion did not play a key role was brewing, and this departure from the norm was due to FDR's great favor of lifting Prohibition. In chapter 4, I examine another economic explanation of the political preferences of business leaders during the New Deal—one that may fare better than mass-consumption theory when region and religion are taken into account.

4

Industrial Structure and Party Competition during the New Deal: The Investment Theory of Politics Reconsidered

This chapter examines another claim about the relationship between specific business sectors and party preferences. Rejecting electorate-based models of political behavior, Thomas Ferguson (1984, 1995) argued that political alignments are based on patterns of allegiance among major corporate campaign contributors who are organized into two industrial sectors: a capital-intensive, internationalist sector and a labor-intensive, nationalist sector. The capital-intensive, internationalist sector (sympathetic to free trade and social welfare) came to dominate the Democratic Party in the 1930s—a domination that only ended when the economic crisis of the 1970s caused this sector to switch to the Republicans (Ferguson 1984; 1995:113–72). According to this view, the multinational bloc's support of the Democrats coalesced in 1936 when the internationalist sector could "be demonstrated to have contributed in hugely disproportionate numbers to the financing of FDR's critical 1936 reelection campaign" (1995:348). Conversely, the nationalist sector, hostile to the rise of labor unions and free trade, put their political investments in the Republican Party.

At first glance, this perspective seems at odds with much of the political history of the New Deal. Although there are many competing accounts of New Deal politics, key interpretations have seen it as a halcyon era of liberal reform (Schlesinger 1960; Leuchtenburg 1963, 1995), or as a time when local elites at the state and city levels influenced the New Deal through administrative control of federal programs (Patterson 1969; Stave 1970; Dorsett 1977; Trout 1977). Others have stressed the role of the state as a "broker" of pluralist competition in the marketplace (Hawley 1966), or as a period when political parties were displaced by special interest groups (Galambos 1966; Badger 1989). Ferguson's emphasis on the way international capitalists attempted to influence New Deal policy has nonetheless received considerable attention (Gourevich 1985; Brody 1985; Noble 1987; Beatty 1995) and, for leftists in particular, his clear and unambiguous emphasis on capitalist dominance of the Roosevelt coalition has enormous appeal despite its economic reductionism.

THE INVESTMENT THEORY OF POLITICS AND THE NEW DEAL

Ferguson sees the events of the 1930s as an example of his "investment theory of politics," which argues that political parties are "defined by major investors who generally have good and clear reasons for investing to control the state" (1995:22). This shaping of the parties by major investors, which basically means organized corporate interests, is a consequence of the limited information, financial pressures, time constraints, and transaction costs that burden most voters. Weak voter control means that blocs of major investors "define the core of political parties and are responsible for most of the signals the party sends to the electorate" (22).

Ferguson does not deny the possibility that organized labor may be a major investor in political parties. Indeed, he agrees that industrial unionism emerged during the New Deal in large measure because working-class Americans organized and pooled their resources in order to influence the political system (1995:82). He notes that unions have been significant investors in other countries, but stresses the relative weakness of American unions and therefore focuses almost entirely on the conflict between national and multinational firms in rival economic sectors.

Ferguson's theory locates firms and industries along two primary axes: "labor sensitivity" and "international market orientation" (1995:118–31). Labor sensitivity refers to the price business will pay for labor compliance, while international market orientation is concerned with the competitiveness of firms in the world economy. Firms that are less labor sensitive and that desire more open international markets are more willing to support a party that favors concessions to workers and unions and endorses open markets and free trade. Some firms have high labor sensitivity, however, causing them to vigorously oppose welfare and unions and favor tariff protection of their industries. Firms are thus categorized as either capital-intensive and internationalist or labor-intensive and nationalist.

If firms cluster in one of the four quadrants created by the labor sensitivity and international market axes (e.g., all protectionist and labor-intensive), then little political conflict will result. But from the 1930s to the 1970s, according to Ferguson, firms tended to concentrate in two diagonally opposed quadrants, with labor-intensive, nationalist firms opposed by capital-intensive, internationalist ones. This produced a relatively stable two-party system in which the labor-intensive, nationalist firms supported the Republicans while the capital-intensive, internationalist firms supported the Democrats (1995:124).

Thus far the model is static. It may clarify the reasons for party competition but it does not explain the periods of critical realignment. According to Ferguson, significant political realignments are caused by fluctuations in the level of national income, which directly affect the primary dimension of labor sensitivity and international economic position. These fluctuations also create "secondary tensions," which place new issues and concerns on the political agenda (1995:126). Economic growth means that firms incorporate new technologies, which decreases their dependence on labor and often creates new industries. The rise of new firms generates tension with traditional industries regarding the primary dimensions as well as in competition for finance. Economic downturns, however, cause far more substantial changes in the party system because they renew economic nationalism, intensify economic rivalries, and provoke conflict over deflationary policies and the choices to be made to stimulate the economy (127–31).

Ferguson argues that economic recoveries are led by "giant, capital-intensive industries which are relatively independent of banks" and which have a great deal of underused fixed capital

(1995:129). Once recovery is underway, however, latent second-ary conflicts emerge, including challenges by new entrepreneurs to the old, competitive pressures brought about by changing financial structures, and infighting among powerful groups. Old alliances begin to break apart—especially among investment and commercial bankers with strong ties to domestic industry. These conflicts tend to obscure the growing importance of the internationalist segment, which seems to be buried in an economic nationalist revival. The spread of economic nationalism among the internationalist bloc is illusory, however, for once recovery is under way the old primary issues begin to reassert themselves.

How does this abstract and economistic model explain the New Deal realignment? Ferguson argues that from 1896 to 1932, the Republican Party was dominated by a major bloc of labor-intensive, high tariff industries allied with the investment and commercial bankers. A few large and powerful firms rapidly developed international markets during the First World War, however, and preferred low tariffs to stimulate international competition, while favoring labor conciliation at home. Allied to this group were the international bankers who had made large loans abroad and were eager for trade and other measures which would stimulate foreign economies (1995:132–34). Ferguson argues that throughout the 1920s the ranks of this mainly Eastern internationalist bloc continued to expand in size and solidify in internal unity.

As a result, the core of the Republican Party's business support began to disintegrate. The economic expansion of the 1920s (which created a tight domestic labor market) exacerbated all the primary tensions over labor and international economic policy, while the capital-intensive firms continued to grow in alliance with the new investment and commercial banks that were opposed to the giant banking interests of the Morgan empire. By the 1928 election, "some investment bankers" (Ferguson names only W. Averell Harriman) and the previously staunch Republican chemical industry had started to move to the Democrats (1995:136–38).

The Democratic candidate Al Smith, however, had rejected the internationalist position while the Republican candidate, Herbert Hoover, had moved toward it—a trend which became more pronounced after 1928 as Hoover was increasingly influenced by the

Morgan banking empire (Ferguson 1995:145). As the Great Depression deepened, industrialists and farmers demanded higher tariffs and the relaxation of antitrust regulations to bring about price stabilization, but Hoover would not accept these policies. His adherence to deflationary policies and the gold standard eventually drove even the most extreme business protectionists from the Republicans to the Democrats.

In 1932, Roosevelt won business support by repudiating his strong support for the League of Nations and making vague commitments to tariff reform and revision of the antitrust laws. Once elected, he also moved quickly to restore confidence in the banking system, which, in Ferguson's view, brought secondary tensions to the fore, splintering traditional alliances. Most importantly, the general hostility to the House of Morgan caused "virtually all the major non-Morgan investment houses" to line up behind Roosevelt (1995:147). The emerging ties between the banks and oil interests created a new financial structure dominated by internationalists—one that quickly came to dominate the Democratic Party.

Ferguson argues that as the New Deal grew more radical, the Morgan-dominated banking community moved against Roosevelt, forcing him to look to industry for allies (1995:149). Many firms (including multinationals, industrialists, farmers, and retailers) were now looking for expansion of purchasing power to restore profitability. Roosevelt's plans for economic recovery were at this stage supported by protectionist industrialists (whose ranks had been swelled by the collapse of world trade), major oil companies, farmers, and the handful of banks not associated with the Morgan group.

This unstable coalition disintegrated, however, as recovery took hold. Capital-intensive firms now looked for ways to resume profitable overseas ventures, moving them toward the international bankers and away from the protectionists who were squabbling over the National Recovery Administration's industrial codes and dealing with labor unrest, especially after Section 7(a) of the National Industrial Recovery Act legalized unions and collective bargaining. Meanwhile, Roosevelt gravitated towards free trade despite the bitter opposition of steel, chemical and other industries, solidifying his support in the capital-intensive sector.

The protectionist and labor-intensive industries, led by a combination of the House of Morgan and the Du Ponts, bitterly opposed the New Deal and sought to use the Republican Party to oppose Roosevelt in the 1936 election. Republicans were ambivalent toward free trade, however, which further alienated the multinationalists at the moment when Roosevelt had opened trade negotiations with other countries and raised reserve requirements, to the delight of the international banks. The Republicans began to desert Landon, and leading Democrats were mobilized in support of Roosevelt, including "a virtual galaxy of non-Morgan banking stars," a large number of oil producers, and such manufacturing interests as R. J. Reynolds Tobacco, American Tobacco, Coca-Cola, ITT, General Electric, Sears Roebuck, and United Fruit (Ferguson 1995:156–57). Roosevelt's victory in 1936 meant that the capital-intensive, internationalist wing of the capitalist class would dominate the Democrats until the early 1970s.

In Ferguson's view, the investment theory of politics allows us to understand the response of business to labor's growing militancy and demonstrates the utility of integrating political and economic analysis (1995:158–9). Because the argument is framed in terms of large firms and industrial sectors and because campaign donations are used as one type of evidence in support of the theory, it is possible to test Ferguson's claims with the 1936 campaign finance data.

INDUSTRIAL SECTORS AND PARTY PREFERENCES

In the original application of the investment theory of politics to the New Deal, Ferguson claimed that tobacco, oil, and chemicals were the most capital-intensive industries while textiles, steel, and automobiles were the most labor-intensive (Ferguson 1984:50). Furthermore, he claimed that "non-Morgan" investment banks and large commercial banks were part of the capital-intensive, internationalist bloc. In a more recent formulation, Ferguson added the food and beverage industry to the capital-intensive sector while restricting the banking sector to the ten largest commercial banks and fifteen largest investment banks—minus Morgan Stanley (1995:220–23). All of these industries will be examined, although particular attention is given to the capital-intensive industries because of Ferguson's claim that they supported the Democrats. As in chapter 3, to establish whether any particular industry was differentially favorable to the Democrats, I used the 17 percent Democratic baseline percentage. This means that if a business sector had a statistically significant percentage greater than 17 percent of donors giving to the Democrats it would initially be considered a Democratic sector.

The investment theory of politics was tested by looking at the donations of all inside and outside directors in the ten largest oil, chemical, steel, and automobile companies; five northern and five southern textile companies matched by size and product; all directors, vice presidents, and second vice presidents in the sixteen largest commercial banks; and all the partners in the fourteen largest investment houses. In table 4.1, we see the percentage of directors in each industry making campaign donations to either party. Once again, the small percentage of contributors is striking.

These industries were analyzed in the same way as the mass-

TABLE 4.1

1936 CAMPAIGN CONTRIBUTIONS OF $100 OR MORE BY OFFICERS AND DIRECTORS OF THE MAJOR CAPITAL-INTENSIVE/INTERNATIONALIST AND LABOR-INTENSIVE/NATIONALIST INDUSTRIES

Industry	Percentage of Contributors	Total Number of Directors
Chemical (10)	48%	178
Steel (10)	41%	201
Autombile (10)	36%	157
Investment Banks (14)	36%	168
Food and Beverage (10)	28%	223
Oil (10)	25%	117
Tobacco (10)	20%	130
Commercial Banks (16)	19%	800
Textiles (10)	11%	135
Totals (100)	27%	2110

Note: Number of companies in each industry is given in parentheses after the name of the industry.

consumption industries in chapter 3. The food and beverage and tobacco industries analyzed in that chapter are included again because Ferguson uses them in his analysis. As seen in table 4.2, only tobacco, oil, and textiles have Democratic percentages much above the baseline for all directors. If only inside directors are considered, then tobacco, oil, textiles, and food and beverage have figures above the baseline percentage. As already shown for tobacco in the analysis of the mass-consumption sector, we shall see that the most important factor in understanding the contributions of the inside directors from the oil and textile industries is region. Southern business executives tended to give to the Democrats while northern business executives gave to the Republicans.

As for the food and beverage industry, it appears higher in Ferguson's analysis because he includes the brewing industry in this category. When it is removed from the analysis, as it should be because of its unique position following the repeal of Prohibition, food and beverage directors are very close to the baseline Democratic percentage. This analysis is strongly supported by the fact

TABLE 4.2

PERCENTAGE OF DEMOCRATIC PARTY CONTRIBUTORS AMONG DONATING
DIRECTORS IN CAPITAL-INTENSIVE, INTERNATIONALIST AND LABOR-
INTENSIVE, NATIONALIST INDUSTRIES (BY TYPE OF DIRECTOR)

Industry	Percentage of Directors	Inside Directors	Outside Directors
Tobacco	42% (26)	36% (14)	50% (12)
Oil	21% (29)	28% (18)	9% (11)
Textiles	20% (15)	25% (8)	14% (7)
Commercial Banks	18% (150)	9% (67)	25% (83)
Food and Beverage	14% (63)	19% (37)	8% (26)
Investment Banks*	10% (62)	—	—
Automobiles	7% (57)	7% (28)	7% (29)
Steel	5% (83)	0% (47)	11% (36)
Chemical	4% (85)	4% (55)	3% (30)

Note: The total number of individuals in each group is given in parentheses. Thus, 42 percent of the 26 directors in the tobacco industry who contributed gave to the Democrats. Industries presented in the table are those used by Ferguson as key examples of the capital-intensive, internationalist and labor-intensive, nationalist sectors of business.

*There is no distinction between inside and outside directors in the investment banking industry because all are considered "partners."

that 87 percent of inside directors in the brewing industry supported Roosevelt while only 19 percent of inside directors in the food and beverage industry did so, illustrating the uniqueness of the brewing industry.

THE CAPITAL-INTENSIVE, INTERNATIONALIST SECTOR

Oil Industry

The importance of region once again becomes apparent when we look at the oil industry, where six of the twenty-nine directors in the ten largest companies contributed to the Democrats (21 percent). Of the five Democratic inside directors, two (H. C. Weiss and E. E. Townes) were born in Texas and another (J. Fletcher Farrell) was born in Missouri and was also a member of the New York Southern Society (a prominent gentlemen's club for Southerners living in New York City). The two remaining inside directors (John A. Brown and Harold F. Sheets) were both with Socony-Vacuum Oil, a Rockefeller company in New York, and do not provide any support for the regional theory. The only Democratic outside director was Walter J. Cummings, a prominent Catholic from Chicago who was chairman of Continental Illinois National Bank and Trust. Region and religion, therefore, loom large in explaining the contributions of four out of six atypical oil directors who gave to the Democrats.

Because the number of inside directors in the top ten oil companies was small, I also looked at the directors of all ninety-one U.S. oil companies listed in *Poor's Register of Directors* for 1936. Although only 15 percent of all outside directors at these oil companies gave to the Democrats (as table 4.3 shows), 32 percent of inside directors did so. When the sixteen inside directors from Texas and Oklahoma are compared with the thirty-nine inside directors from northern oil companies, we find that 50 percent of the sixteen Southerners gave to the Democrats compared to only 26 percent of the thirty-nine Northerners. Put another way, if the sixteen southern inside directors are removed, the Democratic percentage for all oil company directors is only 19 percent, just two percentage points over the 17 percent baseline figure.

TABLE 4.3

1936 PARTY CONTRIBUTIONS BY OFFICERS AND DIRECTORS IN THE
OIL INDUSTRY (BY TYPE OF DIRECTOR)

	Inside Directors	Outside Directors
Democratic	32%	15%
Republican	68%	85%
Total	100% (57)	100% (53)

Note: Number in parentheses shows total number of directors.

$x^2 = 4.13; p = 0.04; r = 0.17$

Thus, any differential support for the Democrats in the oil industry is because of inside directors in Texas and Oklahoma, as Overacker concluded many years ago (1937:487). From this evidence,
I conclude that region is a crucial factor in understanding the
party preferences of the oil industry business leaders who made
campaign contributions.

Thus far, the analysis has focused on the biggest companies in
the oil industry. But was there greater support for the Democrats
among smaller oil firms? The issue of company size is especially
interesting in this industry, where Ferguson makes a distinction
between the "major oil companies" and the "national oil companies" (1995:135). The former are more capital-intensive and because of their move into international oil markets, were certainly
more international in their outlook. The latter group of smaller
companies were much more national in their interests and were
certainly less directly concerned with the vagaries of the international economic system. We should, therefore, find the major oil
companies supporting the Democrats and the smaller companies
supporting the Republicans.

As table 4.4 indicates, however, the major oil companies gave
their contributions to the Republicans, not to the Democrats.
Only six officers and directors out of twenty-nine donors gave any
money to the Democrats and, as we have already noted, four of
these six were either Catholic or southern. Furthermore, only 25
percent of all major oil company executives gave any money at
all to the 1936 Presidential campaign, casting doubt on claims
concerning their political centrality.

TABLE 4.4

1936 CAMPAIGN CONTRIBUTIONS OF $100 OR MORE BY THE OFFICERS
AND DIRECTORS OF THE TEN LARGEST OIL COMPANIES

Company	Number of Directors/Officers	Number/Percent of Contributors	Number Republican	Democrat
Standard Oil (New Jersey)	10	1 (10%)	1	—
Socony-Vacuum Oil (Mobil)	17	4 (18%)	2	2
Standard Oil (Indiana)	12	9 (75%)	9	—
Standard Oil (California)	10	1 (10%)	1	—
Texas Corp.	15	5 (33%)	4	1
Gulf Oil	7	3 (43%)	3	—
Shell Union Oil	12	—	—	—
Consolidated Oil	15	1 (7%)	—	1
Humble Oil & Refining	10	5 (50%)	3	2
Empire Oil & Refining	9	—	—	—
Total	117	29 (25%)	23 (79%)	6 (21%)

Moody's Manual of Investments: Industrial Securities, 1937 lists 122 oil companies, of which the ten largest were classified as "major" and 112 companies as "national." These companies had an enormous range in their net worth—fifty-four were between $1 and 10 million, twenty-three between $10 and 20 million, nineteen between $20 and 60 million, six between $60 and 100 million, and ten between $100 and 190 million. In order to examine party affiliation of officers and directors in smaller oil companies, a stratified sample of 20 percent was taken from each range under $100 million. This sample generated table 4.5 below.

These data indicate that the national oil companies had a higher Democratic percentage than the international companies, the reverse of what would be predicted by the investment theory of politics. The companies with the most Democratic donors among its directors (General American Oil of Texas and Deep Rock Oil of Oklahoma) obviously support a regional theory of campaign donations. Nonetheless, the trend toward Republican is not significantly different for national oil companies, as table 4.6 demonstrates.

TABLE 4.5

1936 CAMPAIGN CONTRIBUTIONS OF $100 OR MORE BY THE
OFFICERS AND DIRECTORS OF "NATIONAL" OIL COMPANIES
(ASSETS BETWEEN $1 AND 100 MILLION)

Company	Number of Directors/Officers	Number/Percent of Contributors	Number Republican	Democrat
Mid-Continent Petroleum Corp.	20	6 (30%)	5	1
Standard Oil (Ohio)	6	—	—	—
Skelly Oil	10	1 (10%)	1	—
Barnsdell Oil	16	2 (12%)	2	—
National Refining	13	2 (8%)	1	1
Quaker State Oil Refining Co.	12	2 (16%)	1	1
Deep Rock Oil	24	3 (12%)	1	2
Plymouth Oil	9	3 (33%)	2	1
Norden Oil	7	—	—	—
General American Oil Co. of Texas	26	4 (15%)	1	3
Messer Oil	13	—	—	—
General Crude Oil	1	—	—	—
Devonian Oil	10	1 (10%)	1	—
Big Lake Oil	8	2 (25%)	1	1
Texon Oil and Land	7	—	—	—
Dominquez Oil Fields	6	2 (33%)	1	1
Italo-Petroleum Corp. of America	10	—	—	—
Total	198	28 (14%)	17 (61%)	11 (39%)

TABLE 4.6

1936 PARTY CONTRIBUTIONS BY OIL COMPANY DIRECTORS,
IN INTERNATIONAL AND NATIONAL COMPANIES

	Republicans	Democrats
International Oil Companies	23 (58%)	6 (35%)
National Oil Companies	17 (42%)	11 (65%)
Total	40 (100%)	17 (100%)

$x^2 = 2.53$; $p = 0.125$; $r = 0.23$

Commercial Banks

The financial sector is the most capital intensive and internationalist of all business sectors, but there is little evidence to suggest that either the commercial banks or the investment banks supported the Democrats to the degree the investment theory of politics would predict. Among commercial bankers, only 18 percent of all directors who contributed gave to the Democrats and among inside directors that figure drops to only 9 percent (well below the 17 percent baseline percentage) with 25 percent of outside directors contributing to the party. Of the twenty-one outside directors who gave to the Democrats, eight were southern, Catholic, or Jewish, and three (Vincent Astor, Cornelius Vanderbilt, and Cornelius Vanderbilt Whitney) were unusual because they came from extremely wealthy families and were not executives in any corporations. Furthermore, they sat on an average of thirteen other corporate boards—far more than usual for that era. These three can be counted along with Southerners, Catholics, and Jews in accounting for the small number of commercial bank directors who supported the Democrats in 1936.

Table 4.7 provides a closer look the commercial bank sector by presenting information about all the directors, officers, vice presidents, and second vice presidents of the sixteen largest commercial banks (each with assets of more than $500 million in 1936). The 800 bankers included in this analysis represent the core of the commercial banking industry in the United States at that time.

Commercial bankers clearly were contributing more heavily to the Republicans. But it is also clear that in banks where the number of Democratic contributors was relatively high, region and religion were significant factors. In the Commercial Illinois National Bank and Trust, for example, Republican and Democratic contributors were evenly split. But the only Democratic inside director (board chairman Walter J. Cummings) was a Catholic, and of the six Democratic outside directors, there was one additional Catholic (meat-packing magnate Edward A. Cudahy Jr.) and two Southerners (Samuel T. Bledsoe and Willoughby Walling). To give another example, of the four Democratic outside directors in the National City Bank of New York, two were Catholic (Sosthenes Behn, the powerful chairman of ITT and Amadeo P. Giannini,

TABLE 4.7

1936 CAMPAIGN CONTRIBUTIONS OF $100 OR MORE BY THE OFFICERS
AND DIRECTORS OF THE SIXTEEN LARGEST COMMERCIAL BANKS (ASSETS
OF MORE THAN $500 MILLION)

Company	Number of Directors, Vice Presidents, Second Vice Presidents & Officers	Number/Percent of Contributors	Number Republican	Democrat
Chase Manhattan	156	18 (11%)	14	4
Guaranty Trust	60	12 (20%)	10	2
National City Bank	21	10 (48%)	6	4
Bank of America (San Francisco)	34	0 (0%)	—	—
Continental Illinois National Bank (Chicago)	47	14 (30%)	7	7
Bankers Trust	55	10 (18%)	10	—
First National Bank (Chicago)	60	26 (43%)	21	5
Central Hanover	49	9 (18%)	8	1
First National Bank (Boston)	51	5 (10%)	5	—
Manufacturers Trust	47	4 (8%)	3	1
Irving Trust	45	9 (20%)	9	—
Chemical Bank	45	8 (18%)	8	—
Security First National Bank (Los Angeles)	44	1 (2%)	—	1
First National Bank	17	7 (42%)	7	—
Bank of Manhattan	52	8 (15%)	7	1
J. P. Morgan Co.	17	9 (53%)	8	1
Total	800	150 (18%)	123 (82%)	27 (18%)

Note: Unless otherwise indicated, banks were located in New York City.

the founder of Bank of America). The industry as a whole did not make significant contributions to the Democratic Party in 1936 and even within individual firms we see that religion and region can explain the presence of Democratic donors.

Investment Banks

According to Ferguson (1995:132), investment banks are a central element in the new capital-intensive, internationalist bloc, so it is reasonable to assume that there would be a significant amount of financial backing for the Democrats from this sector. The work of Carosso (1970:470) made it possible to construct a list of the major investment banks according to the size of the security issues they managed together with a few additional houses regarded as important at this time and mentioned by Ferguson. As table 4.8 shows, however, 37 percent of all partners in the investment banks made contributions, but only 10 percent of these gave anything to the Democrats—well below the baseline percentage.

Only six of sixty-two partners gave to the Democrats and no firm had a majority giving to the Democratic Party. The four investment bankers named by Ferguson in support of his theory (Sidney Weinberg, W. Averill Harriman, James Forrestal, and John Hancock) were the only ones from their firms to make donations to the Democrats (1995:156). Even the companies that Ferguson names as key supporters of the Democratic Party (Dillon Read, Goldman, Sachs, and Brown Brothers Harriman) had a majority of donors giving to the Republicans (1995:156).

Ferguson's analysis is problematic because it makes a key indi-

TABLE 4.8

1936 CAMPAIGN CONTRIBUTIONS OF $100 OR MORE FROM THE PARTNERS
OF MAJOR INVESTMENT BANKS

Company	Total Number of Partners	Number/Percent of Contributors		Number Republicans	Democrats
First Boston	22	1	(4%)	1	0
Dillon Read	9	3	(33%)	2	1
Kuhn, Loeb	10	5	(50%)	5	0
Blyth & Co.	14	0	(0%)	0	0
Edward B. Smith	17	10	(59%)	10	0
Charles D. Barney	20	3	(15%)	2	1
Lehman Brothers	9	4	(44%)	3	1
Brown Brothers, Harriman	9	4	(44%)	3	1
Kidder, Peabody	5	4	(80%)	4	0
Goldman, Sachs	6	3	(50%)	2	1
White, Weld	13	5	(38%)	5	0
Eastman, Dillon	11	5	(45%)	5	0
Drexel & Co.	18	10	(55%)	9	1
Lazard Freres	5	5	(100%)	5	0
Total	168	62	(37%)	56 (90%)	6 (10%)

vidual emblematic of the political disposition of an entire company. In this way, Ferguson views James Forrestal's Democratic contribution as evidence that Dillon Read was a Democratic investment bank (1995:156). Similar problems occur in evaluating other investment bankers. W. Averell Harriman was certainly a Democrat from a wealthy elite family, but Brown Brothers, Harriman was not a Democratic firm because the three other partners who contributed gave to the Republicans, including Averell's brother, E. R. Harriman. Sidney Weinberg of Goldman, Sachs was a big Democratic donor, but the other two partners were not.

Ferguson also draws inferences about the political affiliations of companies from family names. For instance, because Herbert Lehman (the Democratic governor of New York) was once a member of Lehman Brothers, Ferguson (1995:156) infers that the firm was Democratic, when in fact, Herbert Lehman had resigned from the firm in the 1920s. Of the four partners from Lehman Brothers who contributed in 1936, three gave to the Republicans—only Paul M. Mazur gave to the Democrats. One of the Lehman partners named by Ferguson as a Democratic contributor, John Hancock, is not listed as having made any campaign contributions. The evidence is clear: the bankers were overwhelmingly Republican in 1936.

Chemical Industry

The final industry to be examined is the chemical industry. In many respects, it is the epitome of what a capital-intensive, internationalist industry should look like. Chemical corporations spent enormous sums on research and development and were famous for their focus on innovation and their introduction of new, high technology products. According to Ferguson's taxonomy, therefore, it should be pro-Democrat.

In 1936, the industry had the largest percentage of officers and directors contributing (48 percent) but had the smallest percentage of Democratic donors (4 percent), indicating its strongly Republican sympathies. As table 4.9 shows, the ten leading chemical companies were overwhelmingly Republican in their political affiliations, with 96 percent of all contributors giving to the GOP. In the other thirty chemical companies listed in *Moody's Manual*

TABLE 4.9

1936 CAMPAIGN CONTRIBUTIONS OF $100 OR MORE BY THE OFFICERS
AND DIRECTORS OF THE TEN LARGEST CHEMICAL COMPANIES

Company	Number of Officers/Directors	Number/Percent of Contributors	Number Republican	Democrat
E. I. Du Pont de Nemours	43	22 (49%)	22	—
Allied Chemical & Dye	14	2 (14%)	2	—
Union Carbide	10	3 (30%)	1	2
Proctor & Gamble	18	10 (56%)	10	—
Climax Molybdenar	16	1 (6%)	1	—
American Cyanamid	20	14 (70%)	14	—
Texas Gulf Sulphur	9	6 (67%)	5	1
Columbian Carbon	12	7 (58%)	7	—
Hercules Power	12	1 (8%)	1	—
Monsanto Chemical	24	19 (79%)	19	—
Total	178	85 (48%)	82 (96%)	3 (4%)

of Investments: Industrial Securities, 1937, there were eighty-eight
contributors. Of these, seventy-five (85 percent) were Republican
donors and thirteen (15 percent) were Democratic donors. Of
the three Democratic donors in the ten largest chemical companies, two (M. J. Carney and Benjamin O'Shea) were inside directors of Union Carbide, while H. B. Baruch was an outside director
of Texas Gulf Sulphur Co. Benjamin O'Shea was a Catholic from
New York and Herman B. Baruch was the brother of Jewish Democratic financier Bernard M. Baruch. In 1949, Herman would re-
sign his ambassadorship to the Netherlands after a rift developed
between his brother and President Truman (*New York Times* 1953).

Ferguson argues that after 1928 "elements of the arch-national-
ist, previously rock-ribbed Republican chemical industry" led by
the Du Pont family, went over to the Democrats (1995:140). In
order to fund reductions in income tax, Pierre Du Pont suppos-
edly decided that other sources of income would have to be found
for the federal government. Therefore, the Du Pont business empire wholeheartedly embraced the repeal of Prohibition, allegedly to allow the government to levy taxes on liquor and thereby
lower, or even abolish, the income tax. This move was reinforced
by the Du Ponts' ongoing dispute with the Morgan empire and
their concern with competition from the German chemical indus-

try once patents seized in 1918 were returned—a policy favored by the Republicans (1995:140–41). As shown in chapter 2, however, the temporary sojourn of some Du Ponts in the Democratic Party ended acrimoniously in 1934 when they split with Roosevelt over labor policy. By 1936, the whole industry was solidly in the Republican camp.

THE LABOR-INTENSIVE, NATIONALIST SECTOR

Textile Industry

The textile industry is, as Ferguson points out, the most obvious example of a low wage, labor-intensive industry, interested in protecting its economic position through government assistance and high tariffs (1995:120–24). *Moody's Manual of Investments: Industrial Securities,* 1937, lists fifty companies in this sector with a combined worth of approximately $475 million. Only eleven companies were worth more than $10 million and these companies held 51 percent of the total value of the industry. Such figures indicate a reasonably high degree of concentration, but even more important, they show a large number of firms vitally concerned with labor costs.

As table 4.10 indicates, the top firms in the industry did have some contributors, although only about 11 percent of officers and directors made any contribution. Of these, 87 percent made contributions to the Republicans and 13 percent gave to the Democrats. The two inside directors who gave to the Democrats were both Southerners (Charles A. Cannon of Cannon Mills based in Kannapolis, North Carolina, and Cason J. Callaway of Callaway Mills, based in La Grange, Georgia). Cannon, born and raised in Concord, North Carolina, was considered a prominent southern Democrat who was also a director of New York Life Insurance. Callaway, a native Georgian, is a particularly interesting figure. In addition to his industrial interests he also owned Blue Springs, a 25,000-acre plantation in Harris County, Georgia. He was a close friend of President Roosevelt (who was a frequent house guest) and served on the board of the Warm Springs Foundation (Berger 1995). Once again, region seems to explain the few Dem-

TABLE 4.10

1936 CAMPAIGN CONTRIBUTIONS OF $100 OR MORE BY OFFICERS AND
DIRECTORS OF THE TEN LARGEST COTTON-TEXTILE COMPANIES

Company	Number of Officers/Directors	Number/Percent of Contributors	Number Republican	Democrat
Pacific Mills	13	4 (31%)	4	—
Cannon Mills	15	4 (27%)	3	1
Riverside	13	1 (8%)	1	—
Pepperell	10	—	—	—
West Point	9	2 (22%)	2	—
Burlington	9	—	—	—
Callaway Mills	20	1 (5%)	—	1
Berkshire	20	—	—	—
Mt. Vernon	10	1 (10%)	1	—
Nashua	16	2 (12%)	2	—
Total	135	15 (11%)	13 (87%)	2 (13%)

ocratic exceptions to the enormous preference shown for the Republican Party.

Because of the large numbers involved, a random sample of approximately a quarter of the remaining forty-four textile companies was taken. These companies were much smaller in size with total worth ranging from $1 to 10 million. As table 4.11 indicates, the twenty-one contributors from the eleven companies chosen were overwhelmingly Republican. The lone Democratic contributor was Lawrence W. Robert Jr. who came from a prominent Atlanta family and would later be secretary of the Democratic National Executive committee.

Without question, the textile industry dominated the southern manufacturing industry—particularly in South Carolina, North Carolina, Georgia, and Alabama (Martin 1941; Hodges 1986; Cobb 1988). Only the tobacco industry came close to cotton textiles in terms of product value ($57.5 million less than cotton's $911.7 million). Approximately 60 percent of the nation's cotton mills were located in the four main southern cotton states and 73 percent of the industry's labor force was in the South (Martin 1941:162; Hodges 1986:9–10). The southern cotton industry consumed 85 percent of the cotton used in American mills in order to produce 75 percent of the nation's cotton goods (Martin

TABLE 4.11

1936 CAMPAIGN CONTRIBUTIONS OF $100 OR MORE BY
OFFICERS AND DIRECTORS OF SMALL COTTON-TEXTILE COMPANIES
(ASSETS BETWEEN $1 AND 10 MILLION)

Company	Number of Officers/Directors	Number/Percent of Contributors	Number Republican	Democrat
Naumeag	7	2 (29%)	2	—
Victor-Monaghan	14	1 (5%)	1	—
Standard Mills	14	1 (5%)	1	—
Utica & Mohawk	12	1 (8%)	1	—
Consolidated	3	—	—	—
International Cellucotton	10	8 (80%)	8	—
Alabama Mills	25	3 (12%)	2	1
Dunean	11	2 (15%)	2	—
Beacon	7	1 (14%)	1	—
Boott Mills	8	—	—	—
Appelton Mills	10	2 (18%)	2	—
Total	121	21 (17%)	20 (95%)	1 (5%)

1941:164). A major factor in the growth of cotton manufacturing in the South was the existence of cheap labor. In the 1930s, national textile wages consumed 45–65 percent of each sales dollar, but in the South it was 25 percent lower. Although the depression had hit the industry hard, in 1936 it was still the dominant industrial force in the region.

All companies engaged in the textile industry were identified and categorized as northern or southern on the basis of the location of their main operations. This produced a total of fifty-four companies with twenty-nine in the north and twenty-five in the south. Of the companies located in northern states, fourteen had one or more contributors; in the south, fifteen had one or more contributors. As table 4.12 makes apparent, there were no contributors to the Democratic Party presidential campaign from the northern cotton textile industry, located mainly in New England.

In the southern companies there were four Democratic contributors (as table 4.13 indicates), and a number this small cannot represent a significant trend toward the Democrats. The most that could be claimed from these data is that the cotton textile companies located in the north are solidly Republican in their

TABLE 4.12

1936 CAMPAIGN CONTRIBUTIONS OF $100 OR MORE BY OFFICERS AND
DIRECTORS OF COTTON-TEXTILE COMPANIES IN NORTHERN STATES

Company	Number of Officers/Directors	Number/Percent of Contributors	Number Republican	Democrat
Bradley Knitting	8	1 (12%)	1	—
California Cotton Mills	9	1 (11%)	1	—
Continental Mills	7	2 (29%)	2	—
Firestone Cotton Mills	6	2 (33%)	2	—
International Cellucotton	10	8 (80%)	8	—
Manville Jenckes	12	1 (8%)	1	—
Martel Mills	6	1 (16%)	1	—
Merrimack Mfg.	8	1 (12%)	1	—
Mt. Vernon Woodberry Mills	10	1 (10%)	1	—
Nashua Mfg.	16	2 (12%)	2	—
Naumkeag Steam Cotton	8	2 (25%)	2	—
Otis	9	2 (22%)	2	—
Pacific Mills	13	4 (30%)	4	—
Utica & Mohawk Cotton Mills	12	1 (8%)	1	—
Total	134	29 (21%)	29 (100%)	—

campaign contributions. In the south, only a small minority contributed to the Democrats.

Automobile Industry

The automobile industry is classified by Ferguson as a labor-intensive, nationalist industry. In 1936, it had a large percentage of contributing officers and directors (36 percent), but one of the lowest percentages of Democratic donors (8 percent). As table 4.14 indicates, the industry was overwhelmingly Republican in terms of its campaign contributions—as Ferguson's theory would predict. There were only two Democratic contributors among the eighty-seven inside directors (James D. Mooney of General Motors and Walter P. Chrysler of the Chrysler Corporation). Among the seventy-one outside directors, only John C. Hertz and Harold Hirsch (both Jewish) gave to the Democrats. Hertz was an Austrian émigré who founded the Yellow Cab Company and was a

TABLE 4.13

1936 CAMPAIGN CONTRIBUTIONS OF $100 OR MORE BY OFFICERS AND
DIRECTORS OF COTTON-TEXTILE COMPANIES IN SOUTHERN STATES

Company	Number of Officers/Directors	Number/Percent of Contributors	Number Republican	Democrat
Alabama Mills	25	3 (12%)	2	1
Appleton	10	2 (20%)	2	—
Beacon Mfg.	7	1 (14%)	1	—
Brookside Mills	11	1 (9%)	1	—
Callaway Mills	20	1 (5%)	—	1
Cannon Mills	16	4 (25%)	3	1
Columbus Mfg.	10	2 (20%)	2	—
Dunean Mills	11	2 (18%)	2	—
Graniteville	10	1 (10%)	1	—
Monarch Mills	6	2 (33%)	2	—
Pacolet Mfg.	8	3 (37%)	2	1
Riverside & Dan River Cotton Mills	14	1 (7%)	1	—
Thomason Cotton Mills	10	2 (20%)	2	—
Victor-Monaghan	14	1 (7%)	1	—
West Point Mfg.	9	2 (22%)	2	—
Total	181	28 (15%)	24 (86%)	4 (14%)

TABLE 4.14

1936 CAMPAIGN CONTRIBUTIONS OF $100 OR MORE BY OFFICERS AND
DIRECTORS OF THE TEN LARGEST AUTOMOBILE COMPANIES

Company	Number of Officers/Directors	Number/Percent of Contributors	Number Republican	Democrat
General Motors	39	20 (51%)	19	1
Chrysler Corp.	18	10 (56%)	9	1
Hudson Motor	10	2 (20%)	2	—
Studebaker	12	4 (33%)	2	2
Mack Trucks	14	2 (21%)	2	—
White Motor	13	3 (23%)	3	—
Nash-Kelvinator	19	4 (21%)	4	—
Ford Motor	7	—	—	—
Packard Motor	13	7 (54%)	7	—
Yellow Truck & Coach Mfg.	13	5 (38%)	5	—
Total	158	57 (36%)	53 (92%)	4 (8%)

director of Studebaker, and Hirsch was a corporate lawyer and a director of the Atlanta-based Coca-Cola Company.

Steel Industry

The steel industry was another major linchpin of the labor-intensive, nationalist group according to Ferguson (1995:120–24). There were seventy-two companies in the steel sector in 1936 and what is immediately apparent is the astonishing degree of concentration in the industry. The aggregate worth of all steel companies amounted to $4.83 billion, of which ten companies accounted for just over $4 billion—with the giant United States Steel Corporation representing 38.5 percent of the industry total. The ten largest steel companies had a high percentage (41 percent) of contributing officers and directors in 1936, but as Ferguson would expect, only 5 percent gave money to the Democrats. As table 4.15 indicates, the Republican advantage over the Democrats was overwhelming among the larger companies—especially when we consider that all four Democratic contributors were outside directors (James Bruce, Victor Emmanuel, and Jacob F. Schoellkopf Jr. with the Republic Steel Company and Edward A. Deeds with the American Steel Company).

TABLE 4.15

1936 CAMPAIGN CONTRIBUTIONS OF $100 OR MORE BY OFFICERS AND DIRECTORS OF THE TEN LARGEST STEEL COMPANIES

Company	Number of Officers/Directors	Number/Percent of Contributors	Number Republican	Number Democrat
United States Steel	29	8 (28%)	8	—
Bethlehem	17	4 (23%)	4	—
Republic	23	17 (74%)	14	3
Jones & Laughlin	17	14 (82%)	14	—
Youngstown	21	4 (19%)	4	—
National	14	7 (50%)	7	—
Inland	20	10 (50%)	10	—
American	20	13 (65%)	12	1
Wheeling	23	3 (13%)	3	—
Crucible	17	3 (18%)	3	—
Total	201	83 (41%)	79 (95%)	4 (5%)

Emblematic Firms

In addition to looking at the political alignment of various industrial sectors, Ferguson also names specific companies and draws conclusions about their political disposition. This means that companies like General Electric and International Harvester (classified as capital-intensive, internationalist firms) are said to have leaned towards the Democrats, while labor-intensive, nationalist firms like Westinghouse and Du Pont favored the Republicans (1995:135). In fact, of the capital-intensive firms Ferguson names, only twenty-one officers and directors made any contribution to the campaign as opposed to thirty-four from the labor-intensive firms. Furthermore, as table 4.16 indicates, while the labor-intensive firms preferred the Republicans to the Democrats as might be predicted by the theory, it was also true for most capital-intensive firms. Clearly, the capital-intensive, internationalist firms said by Ferguson to lean towards the Democrats showed significant support for the Republicans. Even such stalwarts of the capital-intensive, internationalist sector as General Electric and International Harvester were strongly Republican.

TABLE 4.16

1936 CAMPAIGN CONTRIBUTIONS OF $100 OR MORE BY OFFICERS AND DIRECTORS IN KEY FIRMS NAMED BY FERGUSON TO ILLUSTRATE THE "INVESTMENT THEORY OF POLITICS"

Company	Number of Officers/Directors	Number/Percent of Contributors	Number Republican	Democrat
Labor-Intensive, Nationalist				
Ford	7	—	—	—
Westinghouse	37	13 (35%)	12	1
Du Pont	43	21 (49%)	21	—
Total	87	34 (39%)	33 (97%)	1 (3%)
Capital-Intensive, Internationalist				
American Tobacco	17	2 (12%)	1	1
Standard Oil (N.J.)	10	1 (10%)	1	—
General Electric	20	6 (30%)	6	—
International Harvester	26	12 (46%)	10	2
Total	73	21 (29%)	18 (86%)	3 (14%)

Conclusion

Once again, we have seen that any Democratic preference above the baseline percentage is a function of region and religion—not business sector. According to the official campaign finance reports, capital-intensive, free trade, multinational directors are as Republican as the directors of the labor-intensive, nationalist firms are, unless they happen to be southern, Catholic, or Jewish. Nonetheless, it is possible that some corporations may have found other means to contribute to the Democratic Party in a more indirect and less public fashion. In chapter 5, I will examine one of the biggest controversies in the financing of the 1936 election, namely, the Democratic Convention Book of 1936.

5

Roosevelt's "Soft Money Scandal": The Democratic Convention Book of 1936

To judge from the rhetoric in the 1990s popular media, political candidates today are more immersed than ever before in the murky world of questionable campaign donations. In truth, presidential campaigns have always been fraught with sensational accusations of bribery, "honest" graft, and corruption: paybacks have been a staple of American politics since colonial times (see, for example, Pollock 1926; Thayer 1973; Troy 1997). The Roosevelt years were no exception, as the controversy over money derived from a souvenir book for the Democratic convention of 1936 demonstrates. It was, in fact, the soft money scandal of its day.

To hear the Republicans tell it, the book was a shady enterprise whereby beleaguered business executives were forced to purchase expensive advertisements in the book and then buy massive numbers of copies that they did not want. In fact, the book was perfectly legal and turned out to be an important source of money for the Democrats in 1936, raising approximately $250,000. Any account of campaign finance in this election that did not consider this source would therefore be incomplete, especially because it has been suggested that the financing of the souvenir book was a surreptitious way for top business leaders to support the Democrats without drawing attention (Ferguson 1995:210). The preservation in the National Archives of the financial records for the convention book make a detailed analysis of this controversy possible.

THE DEMOCRATIC CONVENTION BOOK OF 1936:
HISTORY AND BACKGROUND

The Democratic Book of 1936 was not a new idea in American politics. Other presidential conventions, both Democratic and

Republican, had produced souvenir publications to commemorate the event. Indeed, the Republicans also produced a convention "program" in 1936, published by the Cleveland Citizens Committee, who were to receive all profits from its sale (*New York Times* 1936b). These publications were often used by partisans in the host city to generate funds to stage the convention. What was different about the Democratic book in 1936 was that the Democratic National Committee (DNC) both published the book and received the revenues from advertising and sales. The Republicans alleged that the DNC was using the book to raise money illicitly from corporations, in violation of the Corrupt Practices Act of 1925.

The contents of the book were fairly innocuous. The 300-page volume largely consisted of a history of the Democratic Party, the duties and history of Cabinet officers, and an account of the achievements of the Roosevelt Administration. It also had features on Democratic women of the White House, women's activities in the Democratic Party, the story of the White House, Young Democratic clubs, and historic Philadelphia. By guaranteeing a circulation of 100,000 people, the DNC felt justified in fixing a competitive rate for advertising, which was sold for $2,500 per ten-by-thirteen-inch page. The book cost $2.50 for the paperback, $5.00 for the hardback, and $100 for the de luxe edition with Roosevelt's autograph (Michelson 1944:60). After June 1936, when the Democrats had concluded their convention in Philadelphia, the business aspects of the book were placed in the hands of a sales agency (Michelson 1944:61). The agency charged $250 for the leather bound, autographed, de luxe edition.

It was not long before the Republicans cried foul. In October 1936, RNC chairman John D. A. Hamilton urged a special Senate committee investigating campaign contributions to look into the alleged financial irregularities surrounding the Democratic Book. In his view, the Democrats had not only illegally solicited corporate contributions in the guise of advertising and sales but these "contributions" had been coerced. Corporations holding government contracts or having business dealings with the government allegedly had been pressured into making such contributions (*New York Times* 1936c).

In 1937, a special Senate committee headed by Senator Augustine Lonergan (a Connecticut Democrat) ordered the DNC to ac-

count for these practices, and the DNC Treasurer, W. Forbes
Morgan, was brought before the committee to testify. He argued
that sales of the book were perfectly proper and the rates charged
for advertisements were comparable to those charged in any
weekly or monthly national publication. Furthermore, he pointed
out that the Republicans were also charging for sales and advertising in their own convention book. The Lonergan Committee investigation, however, was primarily concerned with whether sales
and advertising amounted to a contribution under the terms of
the Corrupt Practices Act (U.S. Congress, Senate 1937:18). Although the committee did not consider purchases of the book as
such to be in violation of the Corrupt Practices Act, one of the
recommendations in their final report included a broad proposal
to control the sale of advertising or merchandise connected with
presidential campaigns. The political controversy dragged on into
1937 but ended after a Justice Department investigation failed to
find any significant violations of the Corrupt Practices Act.

At the time, there was nothing about the Democratic book that
could be construed as illegal or improper. But this does not obscure the fact that the convention book was a significant source
of revenue for the Democratic Party, although not quite as significant as Republicans claimed. Party receipts show that advertising and sales earned over $860,000, but once commissions on
advertising and sales, printing, and other costs (amounting to
$483,000) are included, together with "a generous allowance for
error and for bills outstanding," the actual net receipts amount
to about $250,000 (Overacker 1937:480). This was no small sum
in 1936 and it merits a more detailed analysis in order to find out
whether corporations used the convention book as a means of
funneling campaign money to the Democrats.

ADVERTISEMENTS IN THE DEMOCRATIC CONVENTION BOOK

Using the 270 largest corporations of the era studied by the Temporary National Economic Commission as an operational definition of "big business," I looked at all firms that either advertised
in or purchased copies of the convention book. With regard to
advertising, between April 1 and December 9, 1936, 143 corpora-

tions paid \$385,525 to advertise their products or services in the convention book, but only thirty-two (22 percent) of the companies that bought advertisements were among the top 270 firms in the United States, as table 5.1 demonstrates. Given that advertising cost \$2,500 per page (Michelson 1944:60), these thirty-two corporations did not inundate the Democrats with advertising revenue. To claim that advertisements are political contributions is debatable and their potential political impact seems to be negligible.

PURCHASES OF THE DEMOCRATIC CONVENTION BOOK

Purchases of the convention book were more lucrative and more extensive than the advertisements. In 1936, a total of 544 firms bought the convention book, but only seventeen (3 percent) were among the top 270 companies in the country. Moreover, as table 5.2 demonstrates, 104 companies bought the book *after* the election. This postelection group of companies includes ten of the seventeen in the top 270. This distinction between purchases before and after the election is crucial, because political contributions made after November 3, 1936 can legitimately be seen as attempts to curry favor with the incoming administration rather than as expressions of political preference. Thus, very few major corporations can be said to have given money to the Democrats via purchases of the convention book.

When we look at the top 270 corporations that purchased the convention book before the election, we have to ask why did such firms support the Democrats when most did not? One possibility is that many of these firms were either headed by religious minorities or Southerners. Inland Steel was owned by the Blocks, a prominent Chicago Jewish family; the Cudahy Packing Co. was owned and operated by the Catholic Cudahy family; Crown Zellerbach was dominated by the Jewish Zellerbachs of San Francisco; Phillips Petroleum was owned by southern oil magnate Frank Phillips, who gave to both parties. As previous chapters and work by Michael Patrick Allen (1991, and Allen and Broyles 1989) has shown for 1936, region and religion are important factors in

TABLE 5.1

TOP 270 FIRMS THAT ADVERTISED IN THE
DEMOCRATIC CONVENTION BOOK (1936)

Company	Date	Amount	Industry
Chrysler Corp.	April 1	7,500	Automobiles*
Schenley Products Co.	April 1	7,500	Brewing
Nat. Distillers Prod. Corp.	April 1	2,500	Brewing
Penn Mutual Insurance Co.	April 3	2,500	Insurance
United States Steel Co.	April 7	5,000	Steel†
Union Carbide Co.	April 10/May 13	2,500	Chemical†
B. F. Goodrich Co.	April 15	3,125	Rubber (Tires)†
Goodyear Tire & Rubber Co.	April 17	3,125	Rubber (Tires)†
Amer. Rad. & Stan. Sanitary Co.	April 18	6,300	Heating/Plumbing
Sears Roebuck	April 25	2,000	Retail
General Electric Co.	May 8	3,125	Electrical Equipment*
Amer. Car & Foundry Co.	May 12	2,000	Railroad Equipment
United Fruit	May 13	5,000	Food Products*
IBM	May 14	2,500	Electrical Equipment*
Firestone Tire & Rubber	May 15	3,125	Rubber (Tires)†
Cudahy Packing Co.	May 15	2,500	Meat Packing
Youngstown Steel Co.	May 18	2,500	Steel†
Standard Oil Co. (NJ)	May 18	2,000	Oil*
American Tobacco Co.	May 21/Sep. 3	5,000	Tobacco*
S. H. Kress & Co.	May 21	1,250	Retail
Phillips Petroleum	May 21	2,400	Oil*
Wilson & Co.	May 22	2,500	Meat Packing
Armour & Co.	May 22	2,500	Meat Packing
Swift & Co.	May 22	2,500	Meat Packing
R. J. Reynolds & Co	May 23/Sept. 25	6,250	Tobacco*
Eastman Kodak Co.	May 26	625	Motion Pictures
Loew's Inc.	June 3	5,000	Motion Pictures
International Harvester Co.	June 30	2,500	Agric. Machinery*
Ford Motor Co.	July 11	4,000	Automobiles*
Paramount Pictures	August 12	2,500	Motion Pictures
Liggert & Meyers Co.	August 17	2,500	Tobacco*
Deere & Co.	October 21	2,500	Agric. Machinery*

Source: Sector based on Ferguson's list (1995:123)

Note: Some industries in this table could not be categorized using Ferguson's list and, curiously, meat packing has a question mark after it and is thus excluded from the capital-intensive sector.

*Indicates capital-intensive or internationalist sector.

†Indicates labor-intensive or nationalist sector.

TABLE 5.2

COMPANIES PURCHASING THE DEMOCRATIC CONVENTION BOOK BEFORE
AND AFTER THE PRESIDENTIAL ELECTION ON NOVEMBER 3, 1936

	Preelection	Postelection
Corporate Purchases	440 (81%)	104 (19%)
Purchases by Top 270 Corporations	7 (41%)	10 (59%)

determining party preference for wealthy donors—and that seems to apply to these instances.

Many of the thirty-six firms that advertised in or purchased the convention book before the election were headed by officers and directors who gave personal donations to the Republicans before November 3, 1936. Specifically, the majority of officers and directors in twenty-seven of the thirty-six firms gave to the Republicans. Four firms were evenly divided between the two parties and only five firms had a majority of officers and directors giving to the Democrats (Union Carbide [chemicals], R. J. Reynolds [tobacco], Cudahy [packing], Schenley Distillers [brewing], and American Car and Foundry [railroad equipment]).

No matter what method might be chosen to resolve the discrepancies between donations by officers and directors on the one hand and advertisements and preconvention purchases on the other, the accumulated evidence on advertisements and purchases casts considerable doubt on the notion that revenues from big businesses are significant. There are not many of such donations, some occurred after the election, and they often conflicted with personal donations from officers and directors.

INDIVIDUAL PURCHASES OF THE DEMOCRATIC CONVENTION BOOK

Corporations were not the only purchasers of the Democratic Convention Book in 1936. The Democratic National Committee receipts show that 557 individuals also bought copies of the book—409 before and 148 after the election. To determine how many of these individuals were business leaders, their names were

TABLE 5.3

TOP 270 CORPORATIONS THAT PURCHASED THE
DEMOCRATIC CONVENTION BOOK (1936)

Company	Date	Amount	Industry
Inland Steel Co.	Apr.29/Oct.23/ Nov.18	2,500	Steel†
Phillips Petroleum	May 21	100	Oil*
F. W. Woolworth Co.	June 1	135	Retail
Cudahy Packing Co.	June 1	250	Meat Packing
Great Western Sugar Co.	September 4	1,500	Sugar
Crown Zellerbach	September 24	1,500	Paper/Pulp*
Amer.Rad.Stan & Sanitary Co.	September 25	5,000	Heating/Plumbing

Purchases after the Presidential Election (Nov. 3, 1936)

Weyerhaeuser	November 12	1,000	Electrical*
California Packing Co.	November 16	1,000	Canning
Continental Can Co.	November 30	500	Indust. Supplies
Ohio Oil Co.	November 30	1,000	Oil*
Swift & Co.	November 30	2,500	Meat Packing
Pennsylvania Railroad Co.	December 7	100	Railroad
Safeway Stores Co.	December 14	1,000	Retail/Food Stores
Allis-Chambers Mfg. Co.	December 15	500	Agric. Machinery*
Youngstown Steel Co.	December 16	250	Steel†
Chrysler Corp.	December 22	100	Automobiles*

Source: Sector based on Ferguson's list (1995:123).

Note: Some industries in this table could not be categorized using his list and, curiously, meat packing has a question mark after it and is thus excluded from the capital-intensive sector.

*Indicates capital-intensive or internationalist sector.

*Indicates labor-intensive or nationalist sector.

checked against *Poor's Register of Directors,* 1936. Only 30 percent of the individuals were found in *Poor's* and only 14 percent of these were officers and/or directors of a top-270 company.

Moreover, as table 5.4 shows, there is a significant difference between those purchasing the book before and after the election. Many important business people in the United States made their purchases of the convention book after the election results had been decided. Specifically, fifteen (65 percent) of the twenty-three officers and/or directors from the top 270 companies who bought the book did so in December 1936. Of the eight who

TABLE 5.4

INDIVIDUALS PURCHASING THE DEMOCRATIC CONVENTION BOOK BEFORE
AND AFTER THE PRESIDENTIAL ELECTION ON NOVEMBER 3, 1936

	Preelection	*Postelection*
Poor's Register of Directors	93 (55%)	77 (45%)
Top-270 Companies	8 (35%)	15 (65%)

bought convention books before the election, only two also contributed directly to the Democrats. Of the fifteen who bought the
convention book after the election, four of them (Frank A. Mer-
rick [Westinghouse], Arthur M. Anderson [J. P. Morgan], James
H. Ward [Bethlehem Steel], and Fred M. Zeder [Chrysler]) gave
significant campaign contributions of at least $3,000 to the Re-
publicans before the election.

DID CAPITAL-INTENSIVE FIRMS FUND THE DEMOCRATS THROUGH THE CONVENTION BOOK?

Although it is doubtful that the advertisements and book purchases were meant as campaign contributions (especially in the
case of companies where top officers made direct contributions
to the Republicans), Ferguson has claimed that a number of big
companies, including such giants as Phillips Petroleum, Signal
Oil, Ohio Oil, R. J. Reynolds, Liggert and Meyers, Lorillard Tobacco, Eastman Kodak, and United Fruit, made contributions to
the Democrats through the convention book (1995:210). It is
clear that Ferguson has combined Democratic revenues from advertising in the book with actual purchases of the book, as table
5.5 shows. These are, as we have seen, very distinct categories.

Furthermore, Ferguson implies that the giant companies he
names are only the tip of the corporate iceberg and that other
large corporate contributors, mainly from the capital-intensive
sector, also used the convention book to contribute to the Democratic campaign. This is simply not so. In terms of advertising,
only twelve firms (37 percent) were in the capital-intensive sector,
six (19 percent) were in the labor-intensive sector, and fourteen

TABLE 5.5

ADVERTISING REVENUES AND BOOK PURCHASES OF COMPANIES CLAIMED
BY FERGUSON TO BE CAPITAL-INTENSIVE CORPORATE CONTRIBUTIONS TO
THE DEMOCRATIC PARTY (1936)

Company	Alleged Corporate Contribution (Ferguson)	$ Amount of Advertising Purchased	$ Amount of Books Purchased
General Electric	2500	3125	—
Standard Oil (N.J.)	2500	2000	—
International Harvester	2500	2500	—
American Tobacco	2500	5000	—
Phillips Petroleum	2500	2400	—
Signal Oil	3500	—	3500
Ohio Oil	1000	—	1000
R. J. Reynolds	3000	6250	—
Liggert & Meyers	2500	2500	—
Lorillard Tobacco	500	500	625
Eastman Kodak	625	625	—
Boeing	2500	—	2500
Grumann	2500	2500	—
Ford Motor Co.	4000	4000	—
Crown Zellerbach	1500	—	1500
IBM	2500	2500	—
United Fruit	5000	5000	—
American, Radiator, Standard & Sanitary Co.	10000	6300	5000

(44 percent) were in neither. When examining purchases of the
convention book, only seventeen companies (3 percent) in the
top 270 corporations purchased the book and ten (59 percent)
made their purchases after the election. Only two companies
(Phillips Petroleum and Crown Zellerbach) could be categorized
as capital-intensive according to Ferguson's criteria and, as we
have seen, region and religion may be more salient variables in
explaining their involvement with the convention book.

CONCLUSION

Although the Democratic Convention Book of 1936 was an important source of revenue for the Democrats, it was not a funding

conduit for giant corporations. As we have seen in previous chapters, American business was overwhelmingly Republican in orientation. Region, religion, and the lifting of Prohibition appear to be the primary predictors of the relatively few Democratic contributors from within the circle of large corporations. This chapter now adds the possibility that smaller companies (such as those who provided revenues from the convention book) may be a significant source of Democratic party support as well.

Given the relatively meager findings up to this point on the financial support for the Democrats, I will next focus on those who did give money to the party in 1936.

6

New York City and the South: The Role of Religion and Region in Financing the 1936 Election

The importance of campaign finance in understanding power during the New Deal era necessitates a move beyond the critical assessment of existing explanations to consider more positive alternatives. If the mass-consumption and investment theories are rejected on empirical grounds, and if the Democratic Convention Book of 1936 was not the conduit for corporate contributions that it has been claimed to be, then what alternative theory better explains the campaign contributions of 1936? The quest for a fully documented account of the sources of financial support for the major parties in 1936 begins in New York City and the South. There are three main reasons why these two locations form a logical starting point for a new explanation.

First, Louise Overacker's analysis of the 1936 campaign finance data argues that the Northeast, including New York City, provided 28.8 percent of all contributions of $100 or more while the South gave 37.8 percent of such donations. By her estimates, approximately two-thirds of all Democratic contributions of $100 or more came from the Northeast and the South (1937:495). Second, as we have seen in chapter 3, contributors in the mass-consumption sectors were largely Jews working in the retail industry. New York City was both the center of the retail industry in the 1930s and contained the highest concentration of American Jews in the nation. Third, the analysis of the investment theory of politics indicated that most of the Democrats in the three business sectors with the highest percentage of Democratic contributors (tobacco, oil, and textiles) were located in the South. Clearly, understanding the pattern of contributions from New York City and the South can provide part of the explanation about who funded the Democrats in 1936.

Both locations embodied many of the starkest contradictions that characterized American life during the Depression. New York City exemplified the prosperous, confident, elegant, and nonchalant world of patrician wealth associated in the popular consciousness with Wall Street and the towering skyline of Manhattan's Upper West Side. But this image was often contrasted with the poverty, unemployment, crime, illiteracy, and squalor to be found in East Harlem, Canarsie, and the Bronx, where glaring social inequalities were often linked to the ethnic divisions that had always given the city its distinctive political character. The agricultural South was seen as the bedrock of the Democratic Party and was generally regarded as having increased its grip on congressional power after Roosevelt's election in 1932. It, too, had its stunning contrasts: a wealthy, white plantation elite and their business allies on one side, and poor, black sharecroppers living in abject poverty on the other.

To set the stage for the analysis of New York City and the South, I drew a random subsample of 1,584 donors from the larger sample used to establish the Democratic baseline percentage. In this national subsample, 65 percent of all donors gave to the Republicans, and these Republican donors were far more likely than Democratic donors to be listed in *Poor's* (43 percent to 16 percent). This can be understood as a correlation of 0.27 between a Republican preference and the business community (chi-square $= 117.25$, significant at the 0.0000 level). In terms of business size, I looked at all the donors listed in *Poor's* who were also connected with one of the 270 largest firms in the United States. Again, there was a significant positive relationship with Republican donations ($x^2 = 4.01$; $p = 0.05$), but the relationship was not as strong ($r = 0.09$). These national findings provide a proper context for understanding the analysis of New York City and the South and also allow us to look at whether business size was a factor.

NEW YORK CITY DEMOCRATS AND CAMPAIGN FINANCE IN 1936

New York City and National Politics

The northern, urban-industrial states were a central element in the electoral strategy of the Democratic Party in 1936. The four great industrial states (New York, Illinois, Ohio, and Pennsylvania) had 135 votes in the electoral college, just over a quarter of the total, while the deep South and border states combined could muster only 179 (Shannon 1948:469). Democratic presidential candidates still courted the South, but it was becoming increasingly apparent that their votes were of less strategic value than those of the industrialized Northeast.

Although many of the northern states had voted Republican during the 1920s, the Republican majorities were rural, not urban, and after 1932 the Democrats were to have significant party pluralities in the urban areas (Eldersveld 1949:1193, 1195). In 1936, the Democrats won all twelve of the largest cities in the United States, providing one-quarter of the Democratic presidential vote. Roosevelt won by margins of 2 to 1 in Baltimore, Cleveland, and Detroit; 3 to 1 in San Francisco; 4 to 1 in Milwaukee; and even bigger margins in the southern cities of Atlanta, Birmingham, New Orleans, and Houston (Leuchtenberg 1995:154). Although the Democrats had started to win urban pluralities with Al Smith, it was Roosevelt who really solidified the Democrats as the party of urban America. In Los Angeles, Smith had won 28.7 percent of the vote in 1928 while Roosevelt received 67 percent in 1936. The Democratic vote jumped in Philadelphia (39.5 to 60.5 percent), Flint (19 to 72 percent), and San Diego (32 to 65 percent) over the same period (1995:155). Cities came to figure prominently in the Democratic Party and none more so than New York.

In 1936, New York City was the largest city in the nation with a population of nearly seven million—more than twice the size of its nearest rival, Chicago (U.S. Bureau of the Census 1933:22). Nonetheless, the Depression had left a profound impression on New York, further accentuating its existing economic and political contradictions. In 1932, the city debt totaled $1.9 billion and revenues from taxable real estate fell drastically as property values fell 25 percent between 1929 and 1933. Unemployment approached 33 percent, and by 1934, 25 percent of New York's expenditures (which totaled $121 million) were welfare payments (Erie 1988:111–12). The city was saved from bankruptcy in late 1932–early 1933 only after a consortium of thirty-four banks put $350 million (repayable at 6 percent interest) into the city. The loan was conditional upon the city administration's guarantees of retrenchment and fiscal "responsibility," imposing further financial strain on the hard-pressed city (Kessner 1989:263).

The severity of the Depression accentuated the move of the metropolis to the Democratic camp. Between 1920 and 1940, New York's proportion of the state electorate grew from 44.1 percent to 51.2 percent (Eldersveld 1949:1192). Although the city had a Republican plurality amounting to 441,000 votes in 1920, by 1928 this had become a Democratic plurality of 454,000 votes. By 1936, New York was voting 3 to 1 for the Democrats, giving them a plurality of 1.4 million votes, more than enough to capture the state's forty-seven Electoral College votes (Eldersveld 1949:1196; Leuchtenberg 1995:154). New York was of crucial importance to the Democratic Party's electoral strategy, but the city was also pivotal—indeed vital—to the Democrats in one other respect: money.

New York City's Campaign Finance Contributions in 1936

Louise Overacker's work on presidential campaign finance provides a useful starting point for examining the contributions made by New Yorkers in 1936. Focusing on the state level, Overacker showed that 74.1 percent of Democratic campaign donations of more than $1,000 came from New York State in 1928 (1932:164–65). In 1932, 69.1 percent of Democratic contributions of more than $1,000 came from the Northeast region, with New York State giving 60.7 percent of these contributions (1933:774–77). The Republicans had 67.1 percent of $1,000–plus contributions coming from New York in 1932, with most of it coming from powerful New York banking and investment houses (1933:775).

Overacker did not make a detailed analysis of the geographical distribution of contributors for the 1936 presidential election.

But as table 6.1 indicates, the Northeast contributed 28.8 percent of $1,000–plus contributions. Because Overacker shows that New York State gave $595,741 to the Democratic Party, we can estimate that the state gave 20.2 percent of the $1,000–plus contributions received by the Democratic National Committee in 1936 (1937:496). Based on Overacker's analysis, the South and New York State provided approximately 58 percent of the Democratic Party's contributions of more than $100 in 1936, although Overacker's rather broad definition of the South (which includes the border states of Maryland, Missouri, and West Virginia) may somewhat inflate the number of southern contributors.

Although these regional data show the importance of New York State to both parties, they reveal very little about the crucial role played by New York City, especially for the Democrats. By disaggregating city contributors, it becomes possible to provide a more sophisticated analysis of the financial role the metropolis played in the 1936 campaign. In fact, 68 percent of the total number of contributors in the state actually came from New York City and 77

TABLE 6.1

GEOGRAPHICAL DISTRIBUTION OF CONTRIBUTIONS OF $100 OR MORE TO
THE DEMOCRATIC NATIONAL COMMITTEE (1936)

Section	Amount Contributed	Percent Contributed
Northeast (Conn., Del., Maine, N.J., N.Y., N.H., Pa., R.I., Vt., Mass.)	847,000	28.8
Center (Ill., Ind., Iowa, Mich., Minn., Ohio, Wis.)	427,870	14.6
South (Ala., Ark., Fla., Ga., Ky., La., Md., Miss., Mo., N.C., Okla., S.C., Tenn., Tex., Va., W.Va.)	1,111,924	37.8
West (Ariz., Calif., Colo., Idaho, Kans., Mont., Nebr., Nev., N.Mex., N.Dak., Ore., S.Dak., Utah, Wash., Wyo.)	188,410	6.4
District of Columbia	146,027	4.9
Other	58,297	2.0
Impossible to Allocate	162,024	5.5
Total	2,941,552	100.0

Source: Overacker (1937:495).

percent of the Democratic contributors in New York State came from the metropolis. As table 6.2 demonstrates, despite the fact that New York City was one of the primary sources of Democratic money, the figures show that the Republicans were still in the ascendancy in terms of contributions—particularly in New York State as a whole. If the Republicans' overwhelming New York advantage had been repeated in other states categorized by Overacker as being in the Northeast, this would have further emphasized the importance of New York City to the Democratic campaign fund in 1936.

Although these data give us some measure of the financial importance of New York Democrats in 1936, they do not tell us who these people were and whether they had any features that distinguished them from Republican contributors. In other words, are there any sociological patterns that might differentiate Democratic and Republican contributors in New York? To answer this question, I conducted a number of analyses to determine if there were any differences between the two groups on the basis of business connections, occupation, religion, upper-class standing, or ties to the urban political machine.

Business Connections and Occupational Backgrounds of New York City Contributors

To find out how connected to business New York campaign contributors were, all 1,409 donors from that city were studied. It was found that 68 percent of the New York contributors gave to the Republicans, while 32 percent gave to the Democrats—a figure

TABLE 6.2

CONTRIBUTIONS OF $100 OR MORE TO THE 1936 PRESIDENTIAL ELECTION CAMPAIGN FROM NEW YORK-CITY AND STATE

	Total Number of Contributors	Percentage of Republican Contributors	Percentage of Democratic Contributors
New York City	1409	68.1% (959)	31.9% (450)
New York State	658	79.6% (524)	20.4% (134)
Total (New York Area)	2067	71.7% (1483)	28.3% (584)

very much in keeping with my findings for the national subsample where 65 percent gave to Republicans and 35 percent to Democrats. Furthermore, the relationship between Republican donors and *Poor's Register of Directors*, 1936 was statistically significant (x^2 = 18.2, p = 0.0000). The correlation is lower, however, (r = 0.12) than for the national subsample (where the figure was 0.27) and for the South because a higher percentage of Democratic donors are listed in *Poor's* (36 percent versus 48 percent for the Republicans). Relatively speaking, the data indicate that New York was more favorable for the Democrats than any other region of the country when it came to contributions from business donors with large firms in 1936.

The notion that New York was a bastion of Democratic support receives further confirmation from the analysis of campaign donors' affiliations with the largest 270 firms in the United States. For Republican donors, the percentage listed in *Poor's* who were also connected with a top-270 firm is 31 percent—eight percentage points higher than in the national sample. For the Democratic donors, however, the figure is 29 percent, more than double their top-270 percentage in the national sample and a figure essentially indistinguishable from the Republicans' (x^2 is not significant). Most of the 47 Democratic and 142 Republican donors from New York listed in *Poor's* and associated with a top-270 firm were, by and large, partners, officers, and directors in the investment banks, commercial banks, retail stores, and manufacturing firms that were examined in earlier chapters. For the most part, Democratic donors occupied a small minority on boards dominated by Republican-supporting officers and directors.

These results confirm the findings reported by Gabriel Almond in his 1938 study of the New York plutocracy. Using membership in leading New York political clubs as an empirical indicator of political affiliation, Almond traced membership in these clubs of the officers of key New York business associations such as the New York Chamber of Commerce (bankers, merchants, industrialists and utility owners), the New York Clearing House Association (commercial bankers), and the Merchants Association of New York (exporters, importers, wholesalers, and retailers). Between 1930 and 1935, Almond found that a large majority of the officers of these organizations were members of Republican political clubs—mainly the Union League and the National Republican Club. There were hardly any business association officers in the Democratic political clubs—a few were in the Manhattan Club, but none in the National Democratic Club (1998:71–76). This lead Almond to conclude that "the Republican Party, particularly in contemporary years, has become the party *par excellence* of the wealthier classes" (1998:73).

Although the knowledge that corporate directors are more likely to be Republican donors than Democratic is useful and interesting, it raises another question: did the Republicans draw financial support from different occupational groups in New York than the Democrats? In order to examine this question, a random sample was drawn of 240 New York Democrats and 240 New York Republicans and compared with the entries in *Who's Who in America, 1936–37,* and *Who's Who in New York (City and State), 1938.* The occupations of the 140 individuals found in these sources were noted from their entries.

The contributors do cluster in certain occupations, as table 6.3 indicates. The most obvious difference is in banking, where there is a larger proportion of Republican donors than Democrat. Republican contributors also outnumbered the Democrats in such occupations as railroads, transportation, coal, insurance, steel and metallurgy, cotton textiles, and chemicals. The Democratic contributors dominated in law and in real estate and construction—industries with strong connections to the Democratic political machine in New York City. The Democrats also dominated the retail industry, manufacturing, publishing, entertainment, public utilities, advertising, medicine, and distilling.

This occupational breakdown of Republican and Democratic contributors in New York coincides with our earlier findings on industrial segments and with similar findings at the national level made by Overacker (1937:485–89), who also suggested that the Democrats represented small business rather than big.

Religion and New York City Democrats

Although most political historians agree that ethnoreligious cleavage has had a profound impact on American political develop-

TABLE 6.3

OCCUPATIONAL CATEGORIES OF REPUBLICAN AND DEMOCRATIC
CONTRIBUTORS IN NEW YORK CITY TO THE 1936 PRESIDENTIAL
ELECTION (BY PERCENTAGE)

Occupation	Republican (N = 73)	Democrat (N = 67)
Banking	31.5%	4.5%
Law	12.2	25.0
Railroad/Transport/Coal	9.6	7.5
Real Estate/Mortgage/ Architect/Construction	5.5	9.0
Retail	4.1	7.5
Oil	4.1	4.5
Publishing	2.7	7.5
Machinery/Manufacture	5.5	7.5
Insurance	5.5	1.5
Steel/Metals	5.5	—
Cotton Textiles	2.7	1.5
Chemicals/Pharmaceuticals	2.7	1.5
Tobacco	1.4	4.5
Entertainment	—	7.5
Public Utilities	—	4.5
Communications	—	1.5
Distillers	—	1.5
Medical	—	1.5
Advertising	—	1.5
Accounting	1.4	—
Art	1.4	—
Education	1.4	—
Sugar	1.4	—
Public Relations	1.4	—
Total	100	100

ment, nowhere has ethnocultural conflict been more prominent than in the Democratic Party (Kleppner 1970, 1979; McCormick 1986; Swierenga 1990; Wald 1997). This was particularly the case in New York, where religion was a major organizing principle of the city's ethnic politics, especially for major, non-Protestant groups such as Catholics and Jews (Lipset 1968; Laumann and Siegal 1971; Ladd and Hadley 1978).

American Catholics   The Democratic Party had emerged as the political home of Catholic immigrants as a result of their opposition to the Know Nothing nativists during the Jacksonian era, when 95 percent of Catholics in New York State supported the Democrats (Benson 1961:187). Catholic support of the Democratic Party declined at the turn of the century as a result of William Jennings Bryan's revivalist appeal to rural Protestants, the effects of economic depression, and the influx of former populists into the party (Jensen 1971; Sundquist 1973; Knoke 1976). Nonetheless, the Republicans were still associated with old stock Yankee Protestants and the Democratic Party remained an attractive political proposition to new immigrants now pouring into the Northern urban cities. In the 1920s, the Democratic Party was increasingly the arena in which tensions between a northern, urban, Catholic, working class came into conflict with a rural, agrarian, Protestant, and white-supremacist southern ruling class (Burner 1968:5–7).

Although Al Smith was badly beaten by Herbert Hoover in 1928, he brought a large number of urban Catholics into the Democratic fold and four years later Roosevelt was to solidify that support into the New Deal coalition (Fuchs 1956; Knoke 1976; Lichtman 1979; Nie, Verba, and Petrocik 1979; Wald 1997). The Democratic Party attracted Catholics because they were grateful to Roosevelt for the welfare measures of the early New Deal and for the patronage that the administration had dispensed. Although Harding, Coolidge, and Hoover had named only eight Catholics to federal judgeships, Roosevelt appointed fifty-one, including the first Italian-American (Leuchtenburg 1995:128; Wald 1997:208–9).

This loyalty to Roosevelt continued in 1936 when white, nonsouthern Catholics showed a significant attachment to the Democratic Party over white, nonsouthern Protestants (81 percent to 52 percent). This relationship holds for Catholics of all socioeconomic groups (only 35 percent of white Protestants of high socioeconomic status outside the South voted for Roosevelt in 1936 while 69 percent of similarly-placed Catholics did so) (Ladd and Hadley 1978:51–53). In general, the evidence suggests that between 70 and 81 percent of all Catholics voted for Roosevelt in 1936, a figure that remained around 73 percent in 1940 and 1944

(Flynn 1968:232–33; Gallup and Castelli 1987:126–27; Leuchtenburg 1995:156). Catholics in New York were a major part of this
urban trend toward the Democrats along with the Irish, Italians,
and other Catholic groups giving significant support. In 1936,
72.8 percent of the Irish and 78.7 percent of the Italians in New
York voted for the Democrats (Bayor 1988:147). Catholics voted
in significant numbers for Roosevelt in 1936 but did they also
support him with money?

In order to examine the campaign finance contributions of
New York Catholics, the *American Catholic Who's Who, 1936* and
1937 was used to find out who the New York Catholics were. This
volume is a comprehensive listing of American Catholics, compiled with the assistance of the Catholic Church and leading
American Catholic newspapers throughout the country. The geographical index lists 370 Catholics in New York City and they were
compared with the campaign finance data for 1936. It was found
that twenty-eight New York Catholics (7.6 percent) had made financial contributions to the 1936 presidential election campaign.
With regard to the party affiliation of these contributors, 71 percent gave money to the Democrats while 29 percent gave to the
Republicans. Although the small numbers have to be treated with
caution, there is evidence to suggest that in both their voting patterns and campaign finance contributions, New York Catholics
showed a marked preference for the Democratic Party.

American Jews   The other major, non-Protestant religious
group in New York City during the New Deal was Jews. In modern
times, perhaps no other group has clung more tenaciously to the
Democratic Party than American Jews. Though they make up only
3 percent of the population, they have provided as much as 6
percent of the national electorate and have successfully reversed
earlier patterns of discrimination to become an important element in the power elite (Isaacs 1974; Whitfield 1986; Zweigenhaft
and Domhoff 1998). They have also been among the most consistently liberal and politically active supporters of the Democratic
Party, providing support both at the ballot box and in generous
financial contributions (Domhoff 1972; Levy and Kramer 1972;
Knoke 1976; Nie, Verba, and Petrocik 1979; Moore 1981; Bayor
1988). In 1968, for example, of twenty-one people giving more

than $100,000 to the party's presidential campaign fund, fifteen were Jewish although in 1972, two-thirds of those who gave more than $100,000 were Jews (Isaacs 1974:122).

With increasing enfranchisement, the political preferences of Jews emerged as an important factor in the electoral calculations of politicians and although they gave some support to the socialist Eugene Debs in 1912 and 1920 and Democrat Woodrow Wilson in 1916, for the most part, Jews were solidly Republican until Alfred E. Smith's presidential candidacy in 1928. Smith addressed many of the concerns of urban Jews such as the support of organized labor, opposition to anti-Semitism, and liberal immigration laws. He also appointed a number of Jews to his campaign and won nearly three-quarters of New York's Jewish vote (Burner 1968:240; Wenger 1996:132). The shift in Jewish political allegiance to the Democratic Party continued in the 1932 presidential election and reached its high point with Roosevelt's landslide victory in 1936 when 86 percent of Jews voted for FDR—a larger percentage than any other ethnic group. Most Jews stayed with the party following Roosevelt's death in 1945 and Jews of all socioeconomic categories continued to vote Democratic (Fuchs 1956:72–74; Campbell, Converse, Millar, and Stokes 1960:159–60; Ladd and Hadley 1978:62–64; Sachar 1992:460; Leuchtenburg 1995:156; Wenger 1996:133–34).

During the Depression years almost two million Jews lived in New York (more than 40 percent of the American Jewish population), making them the largest ethnic group in the city. By the mid-1930s, the Jewish population made up one-quarter of New York's electorate (Erie 1988:119; Wenger 1996:6). The support for Roosevelt by New York Jews grew steadily between 1932 and 1936 and they were the only white ethnic group to increase their support for the Democrats in 1940, as table 6.4 indicates.

This significant transformation in Jewish voting patterns was a result of the following: the economic effects of the Depression, FDR's intervention against the rising tide of fascism in Europe, increasing Republican nativism and anti-Semitism, and the appointment of many Jews to influential positions within the Roosevelt Administration (Fuchs 1956, 1968; Ladd and Hadley 1978; Allswang 1978; Ginsberg 1993). Some scholars have suggested that American Jewish liberalism emerged from the religious pre-

TABLE 6.4

ROOSEVELT PERCENTAGE VOTE IN NEW YORK CITY
(BY ETHNICITY—1932, 1936, AND 1940)

	City	Irish	German	Jewish	Italian
1932	66.4	75.7	62.7	72.2	80.5
1936	73.5	72.8	65.7	87.5	78.7
1940	60.9	56.0	41.8	88.5	42.2

Source: Bayor (1988:147).

cepts of Judaism itself—especially the concern for charity. Beth Wenger, however, has recently argued that secular Jewish concerns with social justice, organized labor, and welfare had far more impact. American Jews had joined radical groups as a result of their ethnic activist tradition and economic hardships brought on by the Depression. New Deal programs relieved the most acute economic distress, so radical groups lost support as American Jews recognized that their political convictions were compatible with the ideology of the New Deal Democratic Party (1996:127–35).

With overwhelming Democratic electoral support from American Jews, it is reasonable to ask whether Jewish campaign contributions to the 1936 presidential election campaign exhibited the same unvarying Democratic partisanship. Both Baltzell (1964) and Domhoff (1972), for example, claimed that Jews became an important part of the Democratic Party (politically and economically) with the onset of the depression in the early 1930s. But the task of discerning the extent of Jewish financial contributions to Democrats during the New Deal is much more difficult at this general level of analysis. This is because the campaign finance data does not record the contributors' ethnicity or religion. Some indicator has to be found, therefore, to provide a reliable way of assessing the salience of Jewish identity as a variable in explaining campaign finance contributions in 1936.

One way of overcoming this difficulty is by the use of name sampling, a technique used in research on numerically small ethnic groups by Himmelfarb, Loar, and Mott (1983) and Lazerwitz (1986). As Himmelfarb, Loar, and Mott report, the use of distinctive Jewish names (DJN) was pioneered by Samuel Kohs in 1942. From the Los Angeles Jewish Federation files, Kohs compiled the most common names appearing in those files and discovered that 106 names accounted for 15.5 to 17.8 percent of the names on the various Jewish Federation lists. Overall, this list of names accounted for 16.24 percent of the total number of names on all the lists used by Kohs. Furthermore, Kohs found that 35 names appeared ten or more times on the lists, accounting for 11.55 percent of all names on all lists held by the Los Angeles Jewish Federation. Between 90 and 92 percent of people with these 35 names were found to be Jewish. By using these 35 distinctive Jewish names, therefore, the percentage of all Jews included is not significantly different from using all 106 names, but the probability of sampling a Jewish person is very high (Himmelfarb, Loar, and Mott 1983:249).

Himmelfarb, Loar, and Mott (1983) conducted a study to find out whether there were any differences between persons with distinctive Jewish names and other Jews. The comparison was made using a number of measures of Jewish identification, including such factors as ritual observance, Jewish organizational participation, association with other Jews, attitudes towards Israel, knowledge and enjoyment of Jewish culture, and attitudes about the Jewish religion (1983:252). They concluded that the difference between Jews with DJNs and other Jews was very small. On the basis of this finding, they argued that "a random sample of persons with DJNs is likely to produce a fairly representative sample of American Jews" (1983:256).

Because of its reliability, the DJN list was used to find out which campaign contributors in 1936 were American Jews. Using the list of thirty-five distinctive Jewish names, we found that there were sixty-five Jews nationally who contributed $100 or more to the 1936 Presidential election campaign. Of these contributors, thirty-three (50.8 percent) were Democrats, twenty-nine (45.3 percent) were Republicans, two gave to progressive organizations (3.0 percent) and one contributor gave to both parties (1.5 percent). In marked contrast to their voting patterns, Jews were fairly evenly divided between the major political parties in their campaign finance contributions in 1936, a finding which casts some doubt on the claims of Baltzell (1964) and Domhoff (1972) that Jews supported the Democrats with the onset of the Depression.

Exactly when Jewish financial support for the Democrats began is thus an open question, but some light can be shed by examining Jewish campaign contributions over the twenty-year period from 1936 to 1956 using the DJN list. As table 6.5 indicates, nationwide Jewish financial support for the Democratic Party only began in earnest towards the end of the Second World War, starting a trend which was to last into the early 1970s (Isaacs 1974; Knoke 1976; Nie, Verba, and Petrocik 1979).

In many respects, the campaign finance contributions of New York Jews in 1936 anticipated trends which were only to emerge nationally in the postwar era. As an initial probe into the campaign contributions of New York Jews, I took the contributors found by using the DJN list and disaggregated the New York City donors from those outside the city. New York City Jews were a significant element in Democratic Party financing, as table 6.6 shows.

Of the thirty-two New York City Jews who contributed to the major parties in the 1936 presidential campaign, 69 percent gave money to the Democrats, a figure that demonstrates their Democratic sentiments. By contrast, most Jews outside of New York City gave to the Republican Party. What the data clearly indicate is that New York Jews were overwhelmingly Democratic in both voting behavior and campaign contributions, unlike the Jewish population nationwide.

As a second probe into the contributions of New York Jews, I used *Who's Who in American Jewry, 1936–39,* a volume that lists the most prominent Jews in the United States for the latter half of the 1930s. All 2,901 names in the geographical index under New York City were compared to the campaign finance data for 1936.

TABLE 6.5

1936 CAMPAIGN CONTRIBUTIONS OF $100 OR MORE BY AMERICAN JEWS
IN SELECTED PRESIDENTIAL ELECTIONS (1936–56)

	Total Number of Distinctive Jewish Names	% Democrat	% Republican	% Other
1936	65	50.8	44.5	4.5
1944	99	80.8	15.2	4.0
1956	90	66.6	33.3	—

TABLE 6.6

PERCENTAGE OF NEW YORK CITY AND NON-NEW YORK CITY
CONTRIBUTORS WITH DISTINCTIVE JEWISH NAMES WHO GAVE $100
OR MORE TO THE 1936 PRESIDENTIAL ELECTION

	New York City (N = 32)	Non-New York City (N = 29)
Democrats	69%	38%
Republicans	31%	62%

Note: Three contributors with distinctive Jewish names were not included in the final re-sults: Ben Cohen of Washington, D.C. gave to the Progressives; Louis W. Kahn of Cincin-nati gave to both major parties; and L. N. Rosebaum gave to the Democrats but his residence was not recorded in the data.

Ninety-eight people (3.4 percent) made contributions—a small number, but one which is supported by the campaign finance literature, which suggests that very few people contribute to politi-cal campaigns. Of those who contributed, fifty-six (57 percent) gave to the Democrats and forty-two (43 percent) gave to the Re-publicans. The data indicate that a strong majority of Jews who might be considered members of the New York Jewish elite pre-ferred the Democrats.

The occupational breakdown of New York Jews can be ascer-tained from the Who's Who in American Jewry, 1936–39, because the geographical index in that volume also includes occupations. As table 6.7 demonstrates, New York Jews who contributed to the Democratic Party were concentrated in legal professions, mer-chandising, and entertainment.

Social Class and the New York City Democrats

In addition to business connection and religion, it was also possi-ble to find out whether the Republican campaign finance donors were more upper class than the Democratic donors. In the United States, a social upper class was formed as successful men reached positions of wealth and power and institutionalized their social position, allowing their children and grandchildren to live "in more or less socially isolated subcultural worlds" (Baltzell 1958:268). During the gilded age, many mercantile and business families married into the old, established families, thus ensuring

TABLE 6.7

PERCENTAGE OF NEW YORK JEWISH CONTRIBUTORS IN
SELECTED OCCUPATIONS (AS LISTED IN
WHO'S WHO IN AMERICAN JEWRY, 1936–39)

	Democrat (N = 45)		Republican (N = 25)	
Brokers/Bankers/Financiers	13.3%	(6)	52%	(13)
Lawyer	27.0	(12)	16	(4)
Merchant	13.3	(6)	8	(2)
Executive	11.1	(5)	12	(3)
Doctor	—		4	(1)
Engineer	—		4	(1)
Manufacturer	4.4	(2)	—	
Diplomat	4.4	(2)	—	
Entertainment	13.3	(6)	—	
Public Official	4.4	(2)	—	
Publisher	4.4	(2)	—	
Rabbi	2.2	(1)	—	
Public Utilities	2.2	(1)	—	
Geologist	—		4	(1)

Note: Number in parentheses shows actual number of contributors.

the continued prosperity and longevity of this socially insulated upper class.

Power and wealth became increasingly concentrated in New York and in 1887 the *Social Register of New York* was first published as a convenient way of allowing members of this upper class to find their friends—both actual and potential. The *Social Register* is an address and telephone book, "a record of society," which can be used as an indicator of social class in the thirteen American cities where the book is published (Baltzell 1958:269). New members are only added upon the recommendation of existing ones—a process still surrounded by secrecy and one which ensures selectivity. Over time the number of entries in the *Social Register* has been pared down so that today it is no longer as reliable an indicator of upper-class standing as it used to be. Nonetheless, for the 1930s, it can still be used as an index of the upper class in America (Baltzell 1958:271–72; Domhoff 1998:78).

I also used *Who's Who in New York, 1938,* which lists prominent people in the city and state of New York. This volume contains information on family background, occupational and military experience, company directorships, fraternal and club memberships, and religious and political affiliations. Both the *Social Register* and *Who's Who* have been widely used in the social sciences as empirical indicators of upper class standing (see, for example, Baltzell 1958, 1964, 1966; Lieberson and Carter 1979; Domhoff 1998).

To look at the upper-class standing of New York City's campaign finance contributors, the same random sample of 240 New York Democrats and 240 New York Republicans was used to ascertain the occupations of New York contributors. Each individual in the sample was compared with names listed in the *Social Register of New York* and *Who's Who in New York, 1938.*

On both measures of upper-class standing, the Republicans outnumbered the Democrats, as table 6.8 demonstrates. This is particularly the case with the *Social Register of New York,* where the Republican donors were more than twice as likely as Democratic donors to have been members of the upper class. In part, this is because Republicans may have been from more established, wealthy families, but it is also a result of the systematic exclusion of various ethnic groups (particularly the Jewish community, who were, as we have seen, key supporters of the Democratic Party in New York). In terms of upper-class standing, therefore, the Republican contributors to the 1936 Presidential election campaign were more upper class than the Democratic contributors in New York.

TABLE 6.8

PERCENTAGE OF DEMOCRATIC AND REPUBLICAN CAMPAIGN FINANCE
DONORS OF UPPER-CLASS STANDING IN NEW YORK CITY (1936)

Source	Republican (N = 240)	Democratic (N = 240)
Social Register of New York, 1937	37.9	15.4
Who's Who in New York, 1938	23	15.4

Machine Politics and the New York Democrats

Any discussion of campaign finance in New York would remain incomplete without some consideration of the Democratic political machine that was the hallmark of city politics for much of the twentieth century. The urban political machine has had a checkered history in social science literature. Initially castigated as a corrupt and undemocratic blight on the American body politic, it has more recently been seen as a complex mechanism of urban immigrant assimilation into the mainstream of American society.

Since about 1870, politics and patronage in New York City was dominated by Tammany Hall, a Democratic political club that was increasingly under the control of Irish immigrants and their descendants (Garrett 1961; Mandelbaum 1965; Callow 1966; Mushkat 1971). Essentially, political machines purchased votes in return for public jobs and services and the distribution of patronage took place within a political environment where ethnic considerations had precedence over building class consciousness or organization (Lowi 1964:34; Katznelson 1981:113; Erie 1988:2). Those who held office as a result of the machine's recruitment efforts were expected to contribute part of their salary to the Democratic treasury and make sizable contributions at election time (Lowi 1964:84; Tolchin and Tolchin 1971:39).

Business leaders maintained a working relationship with the machine because they recognized that Democratic politicians controlled the privileges and protections upon which profit depended (Pound 1935; Lowi 1964; Almond 1998). Yet different businesses were affected in different ways and to different degrees by the actions of city hall—the more regional or local the company's interests, the more involvement they showed in local politics (Gosnell 1937:40; Banfield and Wilson 1967:263; Logan and Molotch 1987). Furthermore, as urban areas expanded, heavy industry moved to areas with cheaper real estate and more accessible water power. The city came to be dominated by small labor-intensive industries, such as textiles, retailing, publishing, luxury goods, etc., which had low, fixed capital requirements and relied on cheap immigrant labor (Stott 1989). These types of businesses needed fiscally responsible city government, efficient public transport, coherent fire and building regulations, and, of course, public contracts. Business leaders had two options: they could work with the machine or attempt to topple it—as they occasionally did with various "reform" movements.

The New Deal did nothing to diminish the importance of the machine and its relationship with city businesses. In fact, "if patronage was the life-blood of the city machines, the New Deal provided a blood transfusion" (Badger 1989:249). Roosevelt ensured that many of the New Deal welfare and relief programs were administered by the city bosses, creating many more patronage jobs for them to distribute (Stave 1970; Dorsett 1977; Erie 1988; Badger 1989). In New York, however, Roosevelt's long-standing conflict with Tammany Hall resulted in his establishing a close relationship with reform mayor Fiorello H. La Guardia, who was "a New Dealer in all but party label" (Dorsett 1977:62). By the late 1930s, control of New Deal programs in New York had allowed La Guardia to seriously challenge Irish dominance of city patronage by providing more jobs and services for other ethnic groups, such as Jews, Blacks, and Italians (Erie 1988; Kessner 1989). Although La Guardia's success was due in no small measure to his ability to unite disparate elements of New York's population, his passing in 1945 allowed the machine to assert itself once again.

The Democratic machine survived because it was able to reform itself in three ways: by incorporating the demands of new ethnic groups, by accommodating business interests, and by colluding with Republicans over patronage. More importantly, although the machine lost control of the upper echelons of city government, it retained control of the lower levels of the city bureaucracy, such as the city council and the judiciary. This control over "everyday government activities" was used "to give the groups and individuals with an immediate stake in city politics what they wanted" (Shefter 1988:146). Business, therefore, still had very good reasons to maintain its relationship with the Democratic machine. As Shefter notes, "Construction firms sought municipal contracts, and real estate owners and developers wanted tax abatements, zoning variances, building permits, and public facilities near their holdings. Building trade unions and mortgage bankers had similar interests. Along with contractors, developers, and realtors, they were the largest contributors to the city's regular Democratic

organizations" (1988:147). The implication of Shefter's analysis
is that it was the smaller businesses in New York that were connected to the machine, especially businesses interested in the
continued growth of the city.

Further evidence connecting the machine to small business is
provided by Gabriel Almond. In his study of the New York plutocracy, Almond (1998:174–77) examined the occupational background of the city aldermen in 1936. The city aldermanic
positions were an important part of Tammany patronage, so it is
reasonable to assume that the office holders were Democrats tied
to the machine. Of the sixty-five aldermen in New York City in
1936, Almond found occupational information on forty-four (68
percent). Twenty-five were categorized as "self-employed"; of
these, twelve were small entrepreneurs (with seven in real estate
and five in small businesses), twelve were in the professions (ten
lawyers, one physician, and one engineer), and only one of the
"self-employed" was in big business. All of the remaining nineteen for which Almond could find occupational data gave an ap-
pointive public office as their occupation. The New York City
aldermen, therefore, were primarily small businessmen and public officials consisting largely of lawyers and people in the real
estate industry.

This analysis of New York City suggests that Democratic contributors were fairly distinct from their Republican counterparts.
Fewer were upper class than their Republican counterparts, they
were less likely to be directors of large and medium-size businesses, more likely to be Catholic or Jewish, and were more likely
to be lawyers, public officials, or realtors than Republican donors.
Democratic contributors, therefore, were in exactly the sort of
religious, class, and occupational categories that would lead us
to conclude that they were more closely tied to the New York
Democratic machine. Although New York City was a stronghold
of Democratic financial support in 1936, the South was also important to the party treasury and it is to a detailed examination of
that region's campaign contributions that we now turn.

The South and Democratic Party Finances in 1936

The South and National Politics

Between Reconstruction and the Voting Rights Act of 1965, the
Democratic Party established single-party rule in the South and

virtually eliminated the Republicans as a political force. Southern white elites, consisting of both planters and industrialists, forged a tacit agreement that modernization and industrialization would proceed, provided rigid racial segregation and white minority rule remained undisturbed (Key 1949:5; Cobb 1988:60; Rae 1994:27–40). The "Solid South" emerged as white elites systematically disenfranchised Blacks and poor whites through poll taxes, literacy tests, and grandfather clauses and made elections mere formalities following candidate selection in white primaries (Cash 1941:128; Kousser 1974:72–81; Black and Black 1987:5–6).

In national politics, the southern wing of the Democratic Party constituted the majority faction in a minority party and their numerical strength in Congress gave them effective control of the party caucus in the House and Senate. More important, the one-party system allowed southern legislators to accrue seniority, which was crucial, as chairmanship of major legislative committees fell to the senior member of the majority party (Potter 1972:44–49). As a result, Southerners headed nearly all key Congressional committees in the early twentieth century, giving them enormous power to obstruct and delay legislation they perceived as being detrimental to the South. At the beginning of the New Deal, Southerners chaired nine of the fourteen most important committees in the Senate and twelve of seventeen in the House— Texas alone boasted nine chairmen of permanent committees (Biles 1994:127; Grantham 1994:122).

In presidential elections, the few white people who voted in the South increasingly voted Democratic. From 1900 to 1936, the South was the most Democratic section of the country, voting Democratic by a 15 point margin over the rest of the country (Ladd and Hadley 1978:43). Southerners were lukewarm over the candidacy of the anti-Prohibitionist and Catholic governor of New York, Al Smith, in 1928, but by 1936 Southerners were once again firmly in the Democratic fold, with 83 percent of white Southern Protestants supporting Roosevelt (Bartley and Graham 1975:12; Ladd and Hadley 1978:51; Black and Black 1987:259–64).

But the effect of New Deal policies in the South was complex and contradictory. Ordinary Southerners embraced FDR with enthusiasm because of their traditional allegiance to the Democrats, Roosevelt's personal popularity, and the South's pressing need for economic relief following the traumatic effects of the Depression. Although the New Deal did bring relief to many, the failure of some states to provide matching funds for federal projects and the reluctance of local elites to interfere with the low-wage economy and racial status quo meant that federal programs did not bring the relief that many poor Southerners anticipated. Ruling elites, however, were more ambivalent about the New Deal's social and economic initiatives. The very programs that caused southern planters to welcome federal intervention (particularly for crop reduction and agricultural mechanization) began to erode their alliance with low-wage industrialists (Tindall 1967:354–60; Biles 1994:18–20; Schulman 1994:3–31; Jones 1998:342). Furthermore, as Roosevelt increasingly courted northern support (specifically organized labor and urban ethnic groups—blacks in particular) conservative Southerners feared that their control of the Democratic Party was slowly ebbing. These tensions were, for a time, submerged as the South threw its support behind FDR's reelection.

The South and Campaign Finance in 1936

In her analysis of the 1936 election, Louise Overacker noted that the South had always been more important financially to the Democrats than to the Republicans. In the 1932 presidential election, the South provided 15.9 percent of Democratic contributions of more than $1,000 but only 4.4 percent of equivalent Republican contributions. In 1936, the South gave 37.8 percent of Democratic contributions of $100 or more, with Texas once again being the largest southern contributor (1933:775; 1937:495). Table 6.9 confirms the South's overwhelming support for the Democrats, with most contributors in *all* Southern states giving to the Democrats. The Republicans garnered some support in Kentucky and Oklahoma, which were border states that had traditionally served as a buffer, dividing the Democratic South from the Republican states in the Northeast, Midwest, and West. They also received money from eastern Tennessee, an area immersed in the traditions of Mountain Republicanism that stemmed from the Civil War period (Black and Black 1992:59). In the deep South, only Alabama fell below 80 percent in Democratic support for reasons I will examine shortly.

In terms of the party preferences of business leaders (given the

TABLE 6.9

1936 CAMPAIGN CONTRIBUTIONS OF $100 OR MORE BY DONORS
FROM THE SOUTHERN STATES*

	Total Number of Contributors	Percentage Democratic		Percentage Republican	
Alabama	65	71%	(46)	29%	(19)
Arkansas	43	93	(40)	7	(3)
Florida	110	86	(95)	14	(15)
Georgia	57	86	(49)	14	(8)
Kentucky	66	67	(44)	33	(22)
Louisiana	95	92	(87)	8	(8)
Mississippi	16	94	(15)	6	(1)
North Carolina	66	94	(62)	6	(4)
Oklahoma	45	62	(28)	38	(17)
South Carolina	101	94	(95)	6	(6)
Tennessee	104	70	(73)	30	(31)
Texas	371	90	(335)	10	(36)
Virginia	65	83	(54)	17	(11)
Total	1204	85%	(1023)	15%	(181)

Notes: Includes southern contributors in both Overacker and Lonergan. Number of individuals is given in parentheses.

*"Southern states" defined as the eleven slave states of the former Confederacy plus Kentucky and Oklahoma.

overwhelming number of southern contributors to the Democrats [85 percent]) it might be expected that a greater percentage of Democratic rather than Republican donors would be listed in *Poor's Register of Directors, 1936,* and that a higher percentage of Democrats would be found in the largest 270 industrial corporations, commercial and investment banks, and insurance companies. My analysis of the 1,121 donors identified as Southerners by Overacker, however, showed that neither was the case. Instead, the correlation between being a Republican contributor and being listed in *Poor's* was positive (0.16), with 27 percent of Republicans being listed in *Poor's* but only 11 percent of Democrats (x^2 = 27.77; p = 0.0000). This indicates that Republicans were more connected to business than Democratic donors. In terms of connections to the 270 major firms in the United States, there was no significant difference between the two parties (8 percent of

Republicans and 7 percent of Democrats had any connection to the largest firms) a finding that might reflect the generally smaller size of most businesses in the region.

Much of the business elite was located in the urban centers of the South, where they had forged political alliances with the commercial, real estate, and banking interests that had brought them real political power in the "New South." In a region dominated by agriculture, it is surprising to find that campaign contributors were heavily concentrated in the cities. In the twenty southern cities with populations of 100,000 or more (Bureau of the Census 1933), sixteen had a majority of campaign contributors giving to the Democrats. Only four cities had a Republican majority and three of these (Louisville, Tulsa, and Chattanooga) were in the more pro-Republican border states, as table 6.10 makes clear. In many cases however, the cities were more Republican than the states in which they were located.

The anomaly of the deep South was Birmingham, Alabama, where the majority of contributors gave to the Republicans. Most

TABLE 6.10

1936 CAMPAIGN CONTRIBUTIONS OF $100 OR MORE FROM DONORS IN ALL SOUTHERN CITIES WITH A POPULATION OF MORE THAN 100,000

Name	Population	City % Dem	% Rep	Total #	State % Dem	% Rep	Total #
New Orleans (La.)	458,762	85%	15%	(39)	92%	8%	(95)
Louisville (Ky.)	307,745	38	62	(29)	67	33	(66)
Houston (Tex.)	292,352	85	15	(47)	90	10	(371)
Atlanta (Ga.)	270,366	85	15	(39)	86	14	(57)
Dallas (Tex.)	260,475	85	15	(52)	90	10	(371)
Birmingham (Ala.)	259,678	42	58	(24)	71	29	(65)
Memphis (Tenn.)	252,143	67	33	(6)	70	30	(104)
San Antonio (Tex.)	231,542	93	7	(28)	90	10	(371)
Oklahoma City (Okla.)	185,389	80	20	(10)	62	38	(45)
Richmond (Va.)	182,929	82	18	(11)	83	17	(65)
Fort Worth (Tex.)	163,447	97	3	(38)	90	10	(371)
Nashville (Tenn.)	153,866	61	39	(34)	70	30	(104)
Tulsa (Okla.)	141,258	40	60	(15)	62	38	(45)
Norfolk (Va.)	129,710	50	50	(2)	83	17	(65)
Jacksonville (Fla.)	129,549	88	12	(16)	86	14	(110)
Chattanooga (Tenn.)	119,798	13	87	(15)	70	30	(104)
Miami (Fla.)	110,637	71	29	(7)	86	14	(110)
Knoxville (Tenn.)	105,802	100	0	(2)	70	30	(104)
El Paso (Tex.)	102,421	100	0	(7)	90	10	(371)
Tampa (Fla.)	101,161	88	12	(8)	86	14	(110)

of these Republican contributors were the executives of the giant coal, iron, and steel corporations, the so-called Big Mules that dominated the city's politics. In the early 1930s, Birmingham depended almost entirely on heavy industry but suffered enormously after manufacturing output in the city fell 70 percent between 1929 and 1933 (Smith 1988:16). Led by Charles DeBardeleben, Hakon A. Berg, and Wade Oldham, the Big Mules became fervent opponents of the New Deal, consistently supporting anti–New Deal candidates for the U.S. Senate. Concerned with the maintenance of the racial status quo and committed to fiscally sound and socially conservative local government, even in the late 1930s they continued to support southern Democrat insurgencies against the party's liberalism but had little success (Biles 1994:135).

Although the largest southern cities were overwhelmingly Democratic in terms of their campaign contributions, they were also very important to southern Republicans, as table 6.11 makes clear. The cities were the center of Republican financial support in 1936 and provided a political base from which the party was able to build in future elections. With wartime industrialization, the

TABLE 6.11

1936 CAMPAIGN CONTRIBUTIONS OF $100 OR MORE FROM DONORS IN THE TWENTY LARGEST SOUTHERN CITIES AS A PERCENTAGE OF STATE DEMOCRATIC, STATE REPUBLICAN, AND TOTAL STATE CONTRIBUTIONS

	Cities as a Percentage of State Democratic Contributions	Cities as a Percentage of State Republican Contributions	Cities as a Percentage of Total State Contributions
Georgia	67%	75%	68%
Oklahoma	50%	65%	56%
Tennessee	40%	87%	55%
Texas	46%	72%	47%
Kentucky	25%	82%	44%
Louisiana	38%	75%	41%
Alabama	22%	74%	37%
Florida	27%	33%	28%
Virginia	18%	27%	20%

expansion of the industrial cities would further contribute to the development of the southern Republican Party in the postwar era.

In general, southern business elites supported the Democratic Party because southern politicians defended the low-wage economy and white supremacy through anti-union legislation, opposition to child labor laws, and strident advocacy of racial segregation. In addition to this, southern political culture regarded it as heretical to vote other than Democratic. Support for the Democrats brought tangible benefits to southern elites, because their control of the legislature enabled them to stymie the encroachment of federal government into southern life. These factors induced many business leaders to contribute according to sectional rather than industrial interests, especially in industries identified with the South such as tobacco, textiles, and oil.

CONCLUSION

New York City and the South were both major centers of campaign finance for the Democrats in 1936, and this chapter has shown that each had very different characteristics. In Northern cities like New York, non-Protestant religious groups, ethnic minorities, city bosses, and organized labor were in the ascendancy. In the South, conservative planters and business leaders were still openly committed to racial segregation and white supremacy. As long as the racial, economic, and political status quo remained undisturbed, Southerners supported the New Deal. But after the 1936 election, as the northern, urban, liberal wing of the Democratic Party came to dominate, the relationship with the South inevitably became more tense and acrimonious.

By 1938, following Roosevelt's abortive attempt to pack the Supreme Court, southern Democrats increasingly found that they had more in common with Republicans then the liberal wing of their own party and conservative southern Democrats and northern Republicans eventually formed a conservative coalition in Congress that was to last until the mid-1960s (Rae 1994:39–40; Domhoff 1998:211). One of the key issues uniting this coalition was the restriction of any further gains by organized labor, which had become an important political and financial force in Democratic politics following the 1936 election. In chapter 7 we will examine the union campaign contributions of 1936.

7

Organized Labor's Political Baptism: FDR and the Unions

One of the most startling developments of the New Deal era was the rapid growth of organized labor. Under the auspices of a more protective and sympathetic state and spurred by a revival of labor militancy, a more radical and dynamic generation of union leaders began to organize the vast number of semiskilled and unskilled workers in the mass production manufacturing industries. The increase in economic power that followed unionization was, by its very nature, political since the New Deal saw the unprecedented politicization of relations between labor unions, business, and the state (Lichtenstein 1989:124). Organized labor assumed a new political significance, and by 1936 it could justifiably claim to be an integral part of the Democratic Party.

The presidential election of 1936 represented organized labor's political baptism. During the campaign, union members not only voted for the Democratic Party, but they also worked the precincts, distributed literature, organized public campaign rallies, conducted registration drives, and generally helped to mobilize new working-class and ethnic voters into the party. The election also saw the emergence of organized labor as a major factor in the financing of the presidential campaign. Indeed, labor contributions were crucial to the success of the party because, as we have already seen, business hostility to Roosevelt had deprived the party of potentially significant sources of campaign funding. This chapter will examine organized labor's rise to political prominence in the 1930s (an important precursor to understanding why union political contributions took the form they did) followed by a detailed analysis of the role organized labor played in financing the Democratic Party in 1936.

The Emergence of Organized Labor's Political Alliance with the Democratic Party

The upsurge in union membership in the 1930s fundamentally changed the nature of organized labor and gave it national political influence that would last until the early 1970s. Although there had been other periods of union growth, this one generated a number of permanent organizations and for the first time, reached out to unskilled and semiskilled workers in the mass production manufacturing industries. The Great Depression initially caused a decline in union membership, which by 1933 was only 2.9 million (a drop of nearly 50 percent from the postwar high of 1919) but union membership rose steadily during the 1930s. By 1935 there were 3.8 million union members and by the end of the decade there were close to 9 million. In 1939, unions organized 23 percent of the nonagricultural workforce—up from just 12 percent in 1932 (Greenstone 1969:41; Levine 1988:111; Badger 1989:118; Zieger 1994:26).

The dramatic transformation in labor's fortunes was due in no small measure to the change in the political environment brought about by the New Deal. Before Roosevelt's election in 1932, capitalists relied on a variety of anti-union measures to ensure labor discipline, including the blacklisting of union organizers, the use of strikebreakers, and outright physical violence. If these measures were not enough, they could also rely on a sympathetic judiciary to issue anti-union injunctions which were backed up by the coercive power of the state. In the name of law and order, state and federal authorities regularly deployed troops to crush strikes, protect scab labor, and keep factories open. While Hoover signed the Norris-La Guardia Act of 1932 that limited the use of anti-union injunctions and outlawed "yellow-dog" contracts (which employed workers on condition they neither joined nor organized a union), Republican administrations continued the attack on organized labor throughout the 1920s and early 1930s.

After Roosevelt's victory in 1932, state pressure on unions eased considerably. Although the incoming Democratic administration did not have any overall plan for labor and although the new president was neither personally nor politically a committed labor advocate, it quickly became apparent that state policy toward organized labor had moved from repression to recognition (Vittoz 1987:78; Finegold and Skocpol 1995:115). Nowhere was this more in evidence than in the passage of the National Industrial Recovery Act (NIRA) in 1933.

The act was designed to stimulate industrial recovery through the creation of the National Recovery Administration (NRA). This new state agency was charged with developing codes of fair competition that would bring together business, workers, and consumers to collectively regulate wages, hours, and working conditions. Each industry was allowed to set its own price and production controls, although in practice codes were established in accordance with "the distribution of the political power that was possessed by each fraction of capital within its branch" (Levine 1988:80). Within months of its enactment, the NIRA was being widely criticized and few tears were shed when the Supreme Court declared the act unconstitutional in June 1934 (Hawley 1966:50–52; Levine 1988:79–87; Badger 1989:88–94). Nonetheless, one particular section of the NIRA was to have an enduring effect on American industrial relations—namely, the labor provisions of section 7(a).

Under section 7(a), all industrial codes had to give workers the right to organize unions and bargain collectively with their employers through representatives of their own choosing without coercion or interference from employers—a provision that business had vigorously opposed during the legislative debate on the NIRA (Vittoz 1987:77–96; Levine 1988:73–79; Domhoff 1990:79–83). Even though section 7(a) was not effectively enforced by the NRA, it sent the message that the government not only wanted workers to organize but would protect their right to do so (Greenstone 1969:47; Finegold and Skocpol 1995:128). Workers were electrified by the apparent promises of section 7(a) and from late 1934 to mid-1935, there was a dramatic increase in union membership and industrial militancy. Although the traditional craft unions grew by only 13 percent, the American Federation of Labor's semi-industrial unions increased by 124 percent and the four major industrial unions grew by a staggering 134 percent (Levine 1988:111).

The emergence of the new industrial unions represented a significant departure for the labor movement because they were committed to organizing all the unskilled wage earners in particular industries rather than organizing workers on the basis similar skills or ethnic affiliations as the traditional craft unions of the American Federation of Labor (AFL) had done in the past. The leaders of the biggest industrial unions (in particular John L. Lewis of the United Mine Workers [UMW], Sidney Hillman of the Amalgamated Clothing Workers [ACW], and David Dubinsky of the International Ladies Garment Workers [ILGW]) quickly grasped the potential of section 7(a) to rejuvenate their struggling organizations. The most spectacular growth occurred in the nation's coal fields. In the early 1930s, membership in the United Mine Workers was under 80,000 but after the passage of the NIRA, Lewis committed money and resources to rebuilding the union. Within a few months, 300,000 new members had joined the miners union, many of them from previously unorganized areas in Pennsylvania, Kentucky, and Alabama (Dulles and Dubofsky 1984:259; Zieger 1994:29).

Union growth in the needle trades was no less impressive. The depression had almost wiped out the International Ladies Garment Workers and the Amalgamated Clothing Workers. In 1933, the ACW (which had 180,000 members in 1920) had dropped to 60,000 with dues being collected from only 7,000. Throughout 1933, the union conducted successful organizing drives in the sweatshops of Connecticut and Pennsylvania and by the end of the year had doubled its membership (Dulles and Dubofsky 1984:259; Fraser 1991:292). The ILGW also saw major gains in membership—particularly in the dress industry—rising from 40,000 in 1933 to nearly 200,000 in May 1934 (Badger 1989:122; Zieger 1994:30).

Labor's gains also extended to industries that had previously been unorganized such as steel, autos, rubber, lumber, etc. But the upsurge in membership overwhelmed the traditional bureaucrats of the AFL who had always been skeptical about the virtues of industrial unionism. Leaders of the old-line craft unions jealously guarded their control of the labor movement and as a result, thousands of new union recruits were initially placed in federal labor unions with direct affiliation to the AFL until jurisdictional issues between the craft unions could be resolved (Dulles and Dubofsky 1984:259; Zieger 1994:32). But the restraint and caution of AFL officials (who criticized new members as undisciplined and inexperienced) were frequently at odds with the enthusiasm and militancy of the newly organized workers who expected action and leadership. With employers fiercely resisting unionization (through company unions and challenges from employer groups such as the National Association of Manufacturers and the American Liberty League) worker disaffection steadily increased.

Labor unrest manifested itself in a precipitous increase in the number of strikes, sit-downs, work slowdowns, and lockouts. Work stoppages and the numbers of workers involved began rising at the end of 1933 and continued unabated into 1935. In 1932, there were 841 strikes involving 324,210 workers; in 1934, there were 1,856 strikes involving 1,466,695 workers; and in 1936, there were 2,172 strikes that involved 788,648 workers (U.S. Bureau of Foreign and Domestic Commerce 1937:331). Working class militancy erupted over demands for higher wages but at least a third of the disputes were over union recognition. In May 1934, auto-part workers of the Electric Auto-Lite Company united with the unemployed of Toledo, Ohio and fought with national guardsmen for control of the city after employers refused to recognize an independent union. In May and June of 1934, violence broke out in San Francisco after police tried to escort strikebreakers to the docks in an effort to break a strike of longshoremen and waterfront workers that had spread to all the major ports on the West Coast. During July 1934, Teamsters fought police after yet another attempt to break the strike. One of the most violent years in labor's history ended in September with a massive strike by textile workers that began in Maine but spread to Alabama and eventually involved nearly one-half million people (Bernstein 1970:217–317; Dulles and Dubofsky 1984:261–64; Levine 1988:117–31; Zieger 1994:33–35).

Labor militancy only added to the continuing and increasingly acrimonious division between craft and industrial unions. In 1934, thousands of union members in the textile, automobile, steel, and rubber industries began leaving the federal unions created by the AFL—disillusioned by the lackluster leadership. Leaders of the industrial unions urged the AFL to organize all workers in a single industry but there was continued intransigence from the craft union leaders—particularly in the building trades. Ostensibly, the conflict concerned organizing strategies but it was also a revolt against the narrow craft economism of the AFL and a demand that labor should play a new role in national politics.

Eventually, by November 1935, those who supported industrial unionism met to set up the Committee for Industrial Organization. Although John L. Lewis of the United Mine Workers took the most prominent role, he was also joined by Sidney Hillman of the Amalgamated Clothing Workers, Charles Howard of the Typographical Union, David Dubinsky of the International Ladies Garment Workers, and Max Zaritsky of the United Hat, Cap, and Millinery Workers (UHCMW), as well as union leaders representing other textile and oil refining workers (Dulles and Dubofsky 1984:278–300; Badger 1989:122–23; Zieger 1995:22–41). Within the needle trades, there was generally more support for the Committee for Industrial Organization from Hillman's ACW, which had only been in the AFL for two years. The ILGW and the UHCMW, on the other hand, were long-standing members of the AFL and were reluctant to make the break. (The ILGW were to return to the AFL in the 1940s and the UHCMW never formally left it [Waltzer 1977:36].) By 1936, the AFL suspended the dissident unions and in 1938 the split in the labor movement was formalized when the industrial unions formed the Congress of Industrial Organizations (CIO)—the organization that would take the lead in the great organizing drives in steel, rubber, and autos in 1936 and 1937.

Worker militancy also contributed to the passage of the National Labor Relations Act (also known as the Wagner Act) in 1935. The limitations in the machinery established under section 7(a) quickly became apparent, especially because employers could not be compelled to engage in collective bargaining with union organizations even if they had won representative elections. When the Supreme Court declared the NRA unconstitutional in May 1935, administration officials and congressional leaders scrambled to find dispute machinery that would prevent labor-management relations from degenerating into outright warfare. By establishing a National Labor Relations Board authorized to hold employee elections based on majority rule, the Wagner Act provided workers with the means of compelling employers to recognize their unions. The act also outlawed company unions and a number of other unfair labor practices (Leuchtenburg

1963:150–52; Badger 1989:120–21; Zieger 1994:35–41). The act was arguably the most important piece of legislation to emerge from the New Deal and was the "only victory for unions in the twentieth-century of any major significance" (Domhoff 1990:104). There has been considerable academic debate on why an act so unfavorable to American business should have passed (see, for example, Tomlins 1985:127–40; Goldfield 1989:1257–60; Domhoff 1990:65–105; Gordon 1994:204–39; Finegold and Skocpol 1995:129–38; Plotke 1996:92–127). But there can be little doubt that the passage of the Wagner Act hinged on the support of southern elites (who gained significant exemptions for southern agricultural labor) and the united action of the craft and industrial segments of the working class.

Despite the emergence of organized labor as a force in Democratic Party politics in the 1930s, there was (strange as it may seem in hindsight) considerable apprehension regarding FDR's prospects for reelection in 1936. Party strategists, therefore, prepared for a real fight and most believed that it would be a tightly contested election. Under these circumstances, party leaders were concerned to secure both the political and financial backing of the rejuvenated labor movement. It is to a detailed analysis of their financial contributions to the election of 1936 that we now turn.

LABOR, POLITICS, AND THE FINANCING OF THE 1936 ELECTION

In the early years of the twentieth century, labor unions lacked any permanent political organization and had few formal connections to the major political parties. Indeed, the AFL strenuously pursued a policy of nonpartisanship and supported protective legislation such as immigration restriction, child labor laws, and minimum wages only as a means to voluntarist ends (Forbath 1991:16–17; Hattam 1993:4–5). As a result, labor unions made minimal contributions to political campaigns, with the AFL spending only $95,000 for political purposes between 1906 and 1936, most of it in the 1920 and 1924 elections (Overacker 1939:57).

In the 1936 election, however, organized labor emerged as a

decisive force on the political scene for three main reasons. First, the labor movement (particularly the CIO) recognized that it was imperative to reelect Roosevelt and a Democratic Congress in 1936 in order to enforce the new labor laws and ensure the passage of further social reforms. Second, labor unions were very concerned about the rise of conservatism (particularly the mobilization of big business against Roosevelt in the form of the American Liberty League and the activities of the anti–New Deal Supreme Court). Finally, CIO leaders were furious when the Roosevelt campaign entrusted Daniel Tobin (the conservative leader of the AFL Teamsters Union) with the task of mobilizing labor support for the Democrats. Thus, despite their previous political affiliations (John L. Lewis was a lifelong Republican who would support Wendell Wilkie in 1940 and both Sidney Hillman and David Dubinsky had voted Socialist in 1932), the leaders of the CIO threw their complete support behind the Democrats in 1936. Nowhere was the political activism of the labor movement more in evidence than in the financial contributions made by the unions to the Democratic Party.

Union contributions were a significant part of the Democratic Party's war chest in 1936, marking a historic shift in the financial base of the party. Organized labor contributed an unprecedented total of $804,456 to the Democratic campaign fund, as table 7.1 makes clear. This figure is greater than the one usually cited by historians and political scientists, who have relied on the figures provided by the Lonergan Committee, which stated that the unions gave $770,324 to the Democrats. After recalculating the dollar contributions listed by the Lonergan Committee, however, I determined that the contributions of Labor's Non-Partisan League had been undercounted by around $600 and, more significantly, the total contribution of the American Labor Party had been undercounted by $33,530.74. The discrepancies are not enormously significant and it may simply be examples of what Richard Hamilton (1996:8) described as an "inertial error," a process whereby historical facts sometimes become part of a citation chain without recourse to the original sources that would enable any correction of factual errors to be made. Nonetheless, one hundred dollars in 1936 would be worth nearly one thousand dollars today. Therefore, in contemporary dollar values, the discrepancy amounts to a shortfall of more than one-quarter million

TABLE 7.1

FINANCIAL CONTRIBUTIONS BY ORGANIZED LABOR TO THE 1936
PRESIDENTIAL ELECTION CAMPAIGN

Name of Organization	Contribution	Percentage of Total
1. Democratic National Committee	$192,550	24%
(a) Direct Cash Contributions	129,879	
(b) Advertising in the Book of the Democratic National Convention of 1936	7,500	
(c) Purchases of the Book of the Democratic National Convention of 1936	4,810	
(d) Loans	50,000	
(e) Reimbursements of portion of expenses for operating sound truck	361	
2. Labor Non-Partisan League	$227,993	28%
(a) National organization	195,993	
(b) State divisions	32,000	
3. American Labor Party in New York	$214,090	27%
4. Roosevelt Nominator's Division	$62,518	8%
5. Progressive National Committee	$40,300	5%
6. Miscellaneous Contributions	$67,006	8%
Total	$804,456	100%

Source: Adapted from the Lonergan Report (1937:127–28).

dollars, but it also underreports the financial contribution made by the American Labor Party to Roosevelt's reelection.

Although a number of different unions contributed to the Democratic cause, it is clear from table 7.2 that by far the largest single contributor was the United Mine Workers union, who gave more than $470,000. This amounted to about 58 percent of labor's total contributions to Roosevelt's reelection. When the contributions of the International Ladies Garment Workers and the Amalgamated Clothing Workers are added, these three unions gave approximately 80 percent of organized labor's financial support for the Democrats in 1936.

Without question, the United Mine Workers were the backbone of labor's newfound political activism. The union had gone into a decline in the 1920s and, deprived of economic power, its political influence had waned considerably. After the passage of

TABLE 7.2

SOURCES OF MAJOR CONTRIBUTIONS MADE BY ORGANIZED LABOR TO
THE 1936 PRESIDENTIAL ELECTION CAMPAIGN

Name	Contribution
United Mine Workers	$470,349
International Ladies Garment Workers	90,409
Amalgamated Clothing Workers of America	62,938
International Alliance of Theatrical Stage Employees and Motion Picture Operators	16,100
Brewery Workers (various unions)	13,013
United Hat, Cap, and Millinery Workers	12,290
International Brotherhood of Teamsters, Chauffeurs, Stablemen and Helpers (various locals)	11,331
Railroad Workers (various unions)	11,151
All other contributions	116,246
Total	$803,827

the NRA in June 1933, the union threw its resources into organizing and the UMW grew at a phenomenal rate, adding 300,000 members in only a few months. After the split with the AFL, the new Committee for Industrial Organizations (CIO) began organizing heavy industry on the basis of industrial unionism and made spectacular gains—often because of the energetic and committed organizing work of communists and other radicals. In June 1936, Lewis formed the Steel Workers Organizing Committee (SWOC) to unionize the steel workers, and in March 1937, labor won a significant victory in the steel industry by forcing the United States Steel Corporation to recognize the union, although the smaller steel companies would prove to be much more resistant to unionization. In the auto industry, workers engaged in dramatic sit-down strikes and factory occupations in January 1937 with the intention of forcing General Motors to recognize the union. After six weeks of violent confrontation (particularly in Flint, Michigan) the auto giant capitulated and agreed to recognize the union (Badger 1989:128–40; Zieger 1994:41–51). War, economic recession, and controversies—both between the AFL and CIO and within each federation—would blunt labor's political activities in the late 1930s and early 1940s, and relations between Lewis and Roosevelt would quickly sour, causing Lewis to move back into the Republican camp in 1940. But this should in no way diminish the significance of the political transformation that Lewis set in motion. After 1936, organized labor moved away from pro-Democratic voluntarism to an intimate partisan alliance with the party (Greenstone 1969:39).

Money was a crucial element in the initial success of the labor-Democratic alliance. In many respects, CIO political support and financial backing for Roosevelt in 1936 grew from labor's recognition that, at a minimum, the acquiescence of the state in labor disputes and its legal protection of collective bargaining were vital to their future success. Lewis in particular recognized that there was an "inseparable connection between New Deal politics and the successful organizing of mass-production workers," and by supporting Roosevelt and the Democrats, he hoped to win for the labor movement the kind of political influence that had eluded it for so long (Dubofsky and Van Tine 1987:195). This is why Lewis threw his time and energy into working for Roosevelt's campaign in 1936 and, more important, why he committed the UMW's money to FDR's reelection.

To fully understand labor's financial contributions, however, it is necessary make a more detailed analysis of the three major organizations through which labor donations to the Democrats were filtered: the Democratic National Committee, Labor's Non–Partisan League, and the American Labor Party. Altogether, these organizations received 79 percent of union contributions to the 1936 election, with much smaller contributions going to both the Progressive National Committee and the Roosevelt Nominators Division.

Democratic National Committee

Nearly a quarter of all union donations were made directly to the Democratic National Committee, where by far the largest individual labor contributor was the United Mine Workers union, which gave $156,350—including cash contributions, loans, and payments (advertisements and purchases) for the Democratic Convention Book. As seen in table 7.3, other, much smaller con-

TABLE 7.3

FINANCIAL CONTRIBUTIONS BY ORGANIZED LABOR TO THE DEMOCRATIC
NATIONAL COMMITTEE (1936)

Name	Contribution
United Mine Workers	$156,350
Cash Contributions	100,100
Convention Book (purchases and advertisements)	6,250
Loans	50,000
International Alliance of Theatrical Stage Employee	
and Motion Picture Machine Operators	15,000
International Brotherhood of Teamsters, Chauffeurs,	
Stablemen and Helpers (various locals)	11,051
Cash Contributions	8,351
Convention Book (purchases and advertisements)	2,700
Railroad Workers (various unions)	3,230
Hotel and Restaurant Employees International Alliance	
and Bartenders League	2,000
Brewery Workers (various unions)	1,453
Other Contributions (under $1,000)	3,466
Total	$192,550

tributions came from the International Alliance of Theatrical Stage Employees and Motion Picture Machine Operators, the International Brotherhood of Teamsters, and the Hotel and Restaurant Employees International Alliance and Bartenders League, as well as contributions from various unions in the railroad industry and the brewing industry.

The Democratic National Committee had organized a Labor Division (headed by Daniel J. Tobin, president of the Teamsters Union and vice president of the AFL) to recruit support for Roosevelt among labor unions. But the protracted conflict within the labor movement over craft versus industrial unionism resulted in CIO leaders resisting any attempts by Tobin to exercise central control over labor's political activities. In fact, the distrust of Tobin by CIO leaders together with their desire to remain independent of the Democratic party organization, were key factors that led to the formation of Labor's Non–Partisan League and the American Labor Party (Savage 1991:96–97).

Labor's Non–Partisan League

Labor's Non–Partisan League (LNPL) was formed in April 1936 by CIO leaders John L. Lewis of the United Mine Workers and Sidney Hillman of the Amalgamated Clothing Workers, together with George L. Berry of the AFL's International Printing Pressmen's Union. It was a distinctively union organization with the immediate objective of reelecting FDR. The LNPL had no formal affiliation with the Democratic Party and, temporarily at least, it bridged the enormous gulf that had opened between the AFL and the CIO (Leuchtenburg 1995:131). Many hoped that the LNPL would turn into an authentic labor party on the European model and some unionists (John L. Lewis in particular) harbored such third-party dreams well into the late 1930s (Danish 1957:93; Epstein 1969:227–28; Waltzer 1977:82–83; Fraser 1991:356–58). Policy controversies would later sour many AFL leaders on the LNPL and they formally left the League in 1938. When John L. Lewis endorsed Republican Wendell Wilkie for the presidency in 1940, the League became a casualty of the subsequent conflict between Lewis and Sidney Hillman (Zieger 1995:179).

At its inception, however, the LNPL had a more statist orientation and attempted to represent the working class as a whole unlike the AFL, which was fundamentally concerned with protecting the labor market interests of a small, white labor aristocracy. The organization was intended to "channel rebellious sentiments into the safe harbor of New Deal democracy," providing a bridge for bringing into mainstream politics hundreds of thousands of unionists who had previously voted Socialist or Communist but who could not yet bring themselves to fully support the Democratic Party (Fraser 1991:362, 367–69). In 1936, the LNPL worked vigorously for FDR's reelection and was a decisive factor in mobilizing voters in the swing states of Ohio, Illinois, Indiana and Pennsylvania (Leuchtenburg 1963:189).

The LNPL also provided 28 percent of organized labor's financial contributions to Roosevelt's reelection, as table 7.4 demonstrates. By far the biggest contributor was the United Mine Workers Union, which gave 76 percent of the total amount raised by the LNPL in 1936. Unions in the New York needle trades (mainly the Amalgamated Clothing Workers and the Interna-

TABLE 7.4

FINANCIAL CONTRIBUTIONS BY ORGANIZED LABOR TO LABOR'S
NON-PARTISAN LEAGUE (NATIONAL ORGANIZATION AND
STATE DIVISIONS, 1936)

Name	Contribution
United Mine Workers	171,978
International Ladies Garment Workers	18,500
Amalgamated Clothing Workers	15,000
United Brewery, Cereal, and Soft Drink Workers	5,000
International Printing Pressmen's and Assistant's Union	2,855
American Federation of Hosiery Workers	2,700
Brewery Workers	800
Brotherhood of Railroad Trainmen	300
Iron, Steel, and Tin Workers	200
Labor's Non-Partisan League of Fayette County	100
Other Contributions and amounts of less than $100	10,560
Total	$227,993

tional Ladies Garment Workers) gave $33,500 to LNPL, 15 percent of the LNPL's donations. Most of the political contributions made by the needle trades were, however, given to the American Labor Party.

The American Labor Party

The American Labor Party (ALP) was founded in July 1936 as the New York State branch of Labor's Non–Partisan League and was initially under the direction of Luigi Antonini, the general secretary of the Italian Waist and Dress Workers Local 89 of the ILGW. The driving forces behind the new organization were the leaders of the New York needle trade unions: Sidney Hillman of the Amalgamated Clothing Workers; David Dubinsky of the International Ladies Garment Workers; and Max Zaritsky of the United Hat, Cap, and Millinery Workers (Danish 1957:93; Leuchtenburg 1995:133). Much like the LNPL, the ALP was specifically aimed at mobilizing workers in New York City for FDR, although it also gathered support from right-wing socialists who had been purged from the Socialist Party in May 1936. Under New York State's electoral laws, a candidate could run with multiparty endorsements and a new party had to receive only 12,000 signatures with a minimum of 50 in each of New York's 62 counties. This enabled American Labor Party voters to cast their ballots for Roosevelt (the ALP's presidential candidate) but have their totals registered separately from those of the Democratic Party (Waltzer 1977:78; Zieger 1995:180).

Interest in the continuation of social reform and the assurance of continued government protection of labor organizing were only part of the reason that union leaders formed the ALP. The Democrats were worried about the large socialist vote in New York City as well as the growing support among urban northern Catholics for William Lemke's Union Party—a strange mixture of progressivism and conservatism backed by Catholic demagogue and radio personality Father Charles Coughlin. In addition to this, Roosevelt feared that "Jews and Italians would stay home rather than vote for their nemesis, Tammany Hall" (Fraser 1991:363). Roosevelt had been at odds with Tammany Hall ever since his support of the Seabury investigation, which had uncovered corruption in the Democratic machine while he was governor of New York. The ALP thus provided a vehicle for independents to vote for Roosevelt without supporting the Democratic machine.

Although the ALP delivered only 274,925 votes for Roosevelt in New York State, it polled 238,845 votes in New York City—about 11.7 percent of the total Roosevelt vote in the metropolis (Waltzer 1977:96). Much of this support came from those who had previously voted socialist and, in districts that were largely Jewish, the ALP vote surpassed the city average. In wealthy Jewish areas on Manhattan's Upper West Side, the ALP gathered only 4.7 percent of the vote, while in lower-middle-class neighborhoods they polled as much as 25 percent (Waltzer 1977:97–100). Following the 1936 election, the ALP continued to play an important role in New York progressive politics and in 1938 helped ensure the reelection of Fiorello La Guardia as the reformist mayor of the city.

But to fully understand the role of the ALP in 1936, it is necessary to look beyond the voting tallies and examine how the party was funded. The ALP received financial contributions amounting to more than $214,000—around 27 percent of organized labor's contributions to the 1936 campaign (see table 7.5). The needle trade unions were the main donors, with the International Ladies Garment Workers, the Amalgamated Clothing Workers, and the United Hat, Cap, and Millinery Workers providing 66 percent of the ALP's funds. The ALP also succeeded in attracting sizable financial contributions from individual members and union locals outside the needle trade.

The biggest union contributions came from David Dubinsky's International Ladies Garment Workers who gave nearly $67,000 (31 percent) of the ALP's total. The ILGW had grown rapidly from 31,000 members in 1931 to 240,000 members in 1936, making it the third largest union in the country. Despite the fact that between 50 and 80 percent of the operatives in the garment and textile industry were women, the ILGW had only one woman among its twenty-three highest elected union officials. The ILGW, like most other labor organizations, would remain male enterprises for many years to come (Stolberg 1944:218–19; Mettler 1998:5, 190). The ILGW was also distinguished by its unique ethnic composition. Union leaders had traditionally organized workers into separate national locals on the basis of ethnic/linguistic divisions, and for much of the union's early history, the vast majority of garment workers were Jews—especially in New York. In 1920, nearly 80 percent of the ILGW's members were Jewish, but by the mid-1930s that figure had declined to 40 percent as second- and third-generation Jewish immigrants moved into white-collar, lower-middle-class occupations (Wenger 1996:15). By 1934, although the union leadership still consisted mainly of Eastern European Jews, 40 percent of the rank and file were now of Italian origin, and successive waves of immigration were to further change the ethnic basis of the union (Stolberg 1944:216; Ortiz 1990:107–14).

In organizational structure, the union consisted of 131 chartered locals and thirteen joint boards located in fifty-six cities throughout the United States (Tyler 1995:210). In many respects, however, the ILGW was a strange hybrid. In terms of organization and culture it remained a craft union, but by the 1930s it had become an industrial union—both ideologically and politically. The heart of the union was in New York City, where each particular craft within the garment industry maintained some autonomy

TABLE 7.5

FINANCIAL CONTRIBUTIONS BY ORGANIZED LABOR TO THE
AMERICAN LABOR PARTY OF NEW YORK (1936)

Name	Contribution
1. International Ladies Garment Workers*	$66,908
Union Headquarters	35,036
Blouse and Waistmakers Union, Local 25	600
Bonnaz and Hand Embroidery Tuckers, Stitchers and	
Pleaters Union, Local 66	1,000
Button and Novelty Workers Union, Local 132	50
Children's Dress and House Dress Union, Local 91	1,300
Cloak and Suit Finishers Union, Local 9	750
Cloak and Suit Pressers Union, Local 35	500
Cloak, Suit, and Infants Union, Local 117	2,900
Cloak and Suit Truck Drivers, Local 102	430
Corset and Brassiere Workers Union, Local 32	500
Dress and Waist Makers Union, Local 22	7,850
Dress Pressers Union, Local 60	950
Italian Waist and Dress Union, Local 89	9,300
Ladies Neckwear Workers Union, Local 142	600
Shirtmakers Union, Local 23	650
Waterproof Garment Workers Union, Local 20	200
Undergarments and Negligee Workers Union, Local 62	1,400
Knitgoods Workers Union, Locals 155 and 2085	105
Textile Examiners and Finishers Union, Local 82	100
Miscellaneous Locals	1,888
2. Amalgamated Clothing Workers	62,432
Amalgamated Bank: (Loans: $10,000; Donation: $25,000)	35,000
3. United Hat, Cap, and Millinery Workers	12,290
3. International Alliance of Theatrical Stage Employees and	
Moving Picture Machine Operators	1,100
4. Furriers Joint Council (inc. Fur Dyers Local 88)	1,300
5. Miscellaneous Unions with Contributions under $1000	
(inc. Teachers, Retail, Painters, Hebrew Butchers, Public	
Employees, Milk Wagon Drivers and Private Individuals)	5,473
Total:	149,503
83,500 contributions, 50 cents each, as membership dues:	41,750
3,161 contributions of less than $100 each:	22,837
Grand Total:	$214,090

Source: Adapted from the Lonergan Committee (1937:132–33).

*List of ILGW's locals compiled from Stolberg (1944); Danish (1957); Epstein (1969);
Tyler (1995).

at the local level, with each local then sending one representative to the Joint Board where collective policies were worked out (229).

As a result of this decentralized structure, many union locals made their own financial contributions to the ALP. Some of the biggest donations came from the Italian locals—particularly the Waist and Dress Union Local 89, which gave $9,300. In the mid-1930s, this was one of the six largest local unions in the country, with a membership of around 37,000, led by the prominent anti-fascist, Luigi Antonini. Local 48 (with its 8500 Italian cloakmakers) also made a sizable contribution of $800. Other large contributions came from predominantly Jewish locals, such as the 26,000 members of the Dress and Waist Presser Union Local 22, who gave $7,850; the 6,000 women members of the Children's Dress and House Dress Union Local 91, who donated $1,300; the 15,000 members of the Undergarments and Negligee Workers Local 62, who gave $1,400; and the 9,000 members of the Cloak, Suit, and Infants Union Local 117, who contributed $2,900.

Among the needle trade unions, the Amalgamated Clothing Workers (led by Sidney Hillman) also made significant contributions to the American Labor Party. The ACW had grown enormously from 60,000 members in early 1933 to around 160,000 by the end of 1934. Under Hillman's leadership, the ACW became an important part of the CIO's attempt to influence presidential politics through the LNPL and ALP, because the union quickly recognized that only the perpetuation and extension of the New Deal could protect the gains the labor movement had made under the Democrats. In support of this objective, the ACW gave more than $62,000 to the ALP. The bulk of this money came from loans and donations made by the Amalgamated Bank—a fully fledged banking institution formed by the ACW at a time when the union was setting up a number of social programs and saw banks as a peaceful way of penetrating the capitalist system. The union actually set up two banks—the Amalgamated Bank in Chicago (founded in July 1922) and the Amalgamated Bank in New York (founded in April 1923). Most union banks collapsed after the financial crash in 1929, but the Amalgamated banks survived largely because of their conservative monetary policies, which somewhat vitiated the pursuit of social and industrial democracy for which they were formed (Amalgamated Clothing Workers 1926:145–53; Soule 1939:143–46; Epstein 1969:160–62).

The third union in the needle trade triumvirate in New York City was the United Hat, Cap, and Millinery Workers Union. Headed by former socialist Max Zaritsky, the union had been formed in 1934 as the result of a merger between hatters and cap makers. In the New Deal labor surge that followed the passage of the NRA, membership in the UHCMW jumped from 19,375 in 1934 to 30,000 by the end of 1936 (Robinson 1948:213–23). The union never matched the influence of the ILGW or the ACW and as fashions changed, it went into a rapid decline in the 1950s. In 1936, however, the UHCMW contributed $12,290 to Roosevelt's reelection, with all money given to the American Labor Party.

The Progressive National Committee and the Roosevelt Nominators Division

The Progressive National Committee and the Roosevelt Nominators Division also benefited from organized labor's financial largesse in 1936. The Progressive National Committee was formed with the intention of encouraging western, progressive Republicans and middle-class liberals to support Roosevelt's reelection. Long concerned with farm relief and suspicious of monopolies, high tariffs and federal intervention, this group of dissidents would later desert FDR over his Supreme Court-packing plan in 1937 (Schlesinger 1960:592–95; Badger 1989:55–56, 266; Savage 1991:113–15). In 1936, however, the Progressive National Committee spent $54,460 and organized labor provided $40,300 with most of the money ($35,000) coming from the United Mine Workers. Unions also made generous contributions to the Roosevelt Nominators Division. This organization was formed with the intention of persuading individuals to become "nominators" by contributing $1 to the campaign fund and it eventually handed over $809,190 to the Democratic National Committee (Overacker 1937:478–79). Labor gave $62,517 to the Roosevelt Nominators with the bulk of the money ($50,480) coming once again from the United Mine Workers.

CONCLUSION

Organized labor formed an alliance with the Democratic Party in 1936 that placed it in the national political arena for the first time. A new generation of labor leaders emerged in the 1930s that recognized how important political participation in the party was to secure the gains they had made under the New Deal. Just eight years later (based upon a survey of top trade unionists), C. Wright Mills reported that although 72 percent of all union leaders belonged to one of the major parties, AFL leaders were Republican in a five-to-one margin over CIO leaders. AFL leaders were mostly Democrat (54 percent), with 22 percent Republican, 18 percent independent, 3 percent socialist, and 3 percent in third parties. CIO leaders were 58 percent Democrat, but the American Labor Party came in second with 19 percent. The Independent Party accounted for 9 percent of CIO leaders, with third-party membership at 6 percent, Republican at only 5 percent, and the Socialist Party trailing at 3 percent (1979:90–91). The partisan alliance between organized labor and the Democratic Party endured well beyond 1936, and this fact receives further confirmation in union political behavior studies by Greenstone (1969) and Form (1995)—although by the 1990s the relationship was somewhat strained.

One of the most important elements of that alliance was money. The unions gave more than $800,000 to Roosevelt's war chest in 1936, but relatively little of this went directly to the Democratic Party. Labor designed innovative new strategies to maximize their bargaining power—setting up new institutions to funnel money into the campaign. Recognizing the political realities both within their own unions and the Democratic Party itself, Labor's Non–Partisan League, the American Labor Party, the Progressive National Committee, and the Roosevelt Nominators Division became important conduits for union money to support Roosevelt's reelection campaign. These organizations also provided an important bridge by which union members with more socialist, radical, or progressive sympathies could support FDR. Finally, they gave the CIO leadership a way to circumvent resistance anticipated from the AFL leaders who were coordinating labor's relations with the Democratic Party.

8

Conclusion

The presidential election of 1936 was, in many respects, a referendum on the activist role taken by the federal government since the inception of the New Deal. The minimalist state that dominated American politics in the early part of the twentieth century was abandoned as the government acted to mitigate the worst effects of industrial capitalism and restore some measure of economic and social justice. The new welfare state that emerged guaranteed union rights and collective bargaining, regulated wages and hours, provided a safety net for those who were retired, unemployed, or disabled, and stabilized agricultural prices. More important, the New Deal (for one of the few times in American history) broke the monopoly on political power long held "by those who happened to be rich, white, male, Anglo-Saxon, Protestant, and members of the business community" (Parrish 1992:391).

The "New Deal coalition" that reelected Roosevelt was made up of the southern segment of the ruling class together with various groups (organized labor, religious and ethnic minorities, the urban poor, liberals, and progressives) who previously had been outside the mainstream of the American power structure. This coalition ensured Roosevelt a second term in 1936 by giving him 60.8 percent of the vote (the highest in American history) and a plurality of eleven million votes over Republican challenger Herbert Hoover. As noted earlier, Roosevelt won 76 percent of the southern vote, 80 percent of the labor vote, 86 percent of the Jewish vote, as much as 81 percent of the Catholic vote, and 76 percent of the black vote in the northern cities (Sachar 1992:460; Leuchtenburg 1995:145–57).

Although the voting data point to the electoral strength of the New Deal coalition, one other critically important component of the coalition's triumph in 1936 has usually been overlooked; namely, the sources of Democratic campaign finance. Given the hostility of most big business leaders to the New Deal agenda, Democrats could not expect to garner much financial support from that direction. In fact, as this study has shown, most business sectors were heavily Republican in terms of their campaign contributions. It is religion, region, organized labor, and the lifting of Prohibition that best explain the greater tendency to contribute to the Democrats. This conclusion suggests that campaign contributions in 1936 are best understood by what social scientists and historians have learned about New Deal political parties: namely, that while the Republicans remained the party of big business, the Democrats forged a new coalition based on the South, organized labor, Catholics, Jews, and small business. As Louise Overacker concluded in her studies of New Deal campaign finance, "the further one goes into the financial backing of the two parties the more convincing is the evidence that they receive their support from very different groups, with what might even be called distinct characteristics" (1945:915).

Nonetheless, this conclusion is in marked contrast to the investment theory of politics, which essentially argues that a multinational bloc seized control of the Democratic Party in 1936 and subsequently shaped the programs and policies of the New Deal. It also opposes the arguments forwarded by mass-consumption theorists purporting to show that industries needing high levels of consumer demand supported the Democrats. Both of these theories are led astray because they overstate the preference of top business leaders for the Democrats for two main reasons. First, their focus is mainly on New York where there was a higher percentage of Democratic business donors in *Poor's* and top–270 firms than in the country as a whole or in the South. Second, because they often argue from emblematic examples of important Democrats in the business community, they are overly focused on the forty-seven Democratic contributors from New York City who were connected to top–270 firms. With the Keynesian elite named by Friedlander (1987), for example, eight of nineteen Democrats (42 percent) were from the atypical forty-seven, while of the capital-intensive sectors named by Ferguson (1984), twenty of forty-seven (43 percent) were from the list of big, New York Democrats.

On the other hand, much of this analysis generally supports

Louise Overacker's contention that American business was the financial backbone of the Republican Party. Overacker's findings were based upon a detailed, comprehensive, and painstaking examination of the campaign finance data and her general conclusions should be an integral part of any study of political power in the 1930s. Nonetheless, her claim that the bankers and financiers deserted the Democrats is based on a misreading of the data. Any desertions from the Democratic Party in 1936 were by members of the Du Pont business network together with some dissident, conservative, nonbusiness Democrats whose party loyalty had been tenuous since the early 1930s.

Although the findings in this book do not support any of the claims made by the investment theory of politics, the mass-consumption theorists, or the bankers' revolt thesis, they are highly compatible with other findings on the history and financing of the two major parties. First, they support Overacker's neglected conclusion that the Democrats were supported by southern businessmen and smaller businesses outside the South, as well as lawyers, office holders, and organized labor. Except for her often-cited claim about the bankers, her conclusions about the financing of the Democratic Party have stood the test of time.

Second, these findings are compatible with those of Michael Patrick Allen (1991) on the 1936 campaign donations of wealthy families and by the "inner circle" of top corporate executives in that era. Allen estimated that about 80 percent of the major capitalists who contributed to the 1936 presidential campaign gave to the Republicans. This means that approximately 20 percent gave to the Democrats, a figure very close to the 17 percent baseline percentage taken from the *Poor's* sample. Furthermore, Allen argues that "socially marginal, 'out-groups' like Southerners and Jews were much more supportive of the Democratic Party" (1991:687).

Third, these results are consistent with the findings reported by Gabriel Almond (1998) in his study of the New York plutocracy in the 1930s. Using membership in leading New York political clubs as an indicator of political affiliation, Almond found that while a large majority of New York business leaders were members of Republican political clubs, there were hardly any business leaders in the Democratic political clubs. This led him to conclude

that in the 1930s, the Republican Party had become the party of
the wealthier classes (1998:73). Almond also suggested that the
plutocracy had never really been Democratic and would seek the
most effective means to defend its privileged position even if it
meant supporting vigilantist and profascist groups. In fact, Almond argued, American politics would "continue to be animated
by an intensifying struggle between the wealthier classes and
those elements seeking a greater share in the fruits of our economy and technique" (1998:240).

Fourth, the findings on the religious differences regarding the
party preferences of business leaders in mass-consumption industries are compatible with those of Alexander (1971) for the donations of New York businessmen in 1948 and 1952; of national
surveys of the general population for 1952, 1956, and 1960
(Heard 1962:424); and of Domhoff (1990:225–55) for the 1968
and 1984 elections. These studies suggest that businessmen from
the Jewish community favor the Democratic Party. Some observ-
ers (e.g., Isaacs 1974; Cohen 1989; Lipset and Raab 1995) estimate that members of the Jewish community have come to
provide Democrats outside the South with as much as half of their
financial support.

Fifth, the results are compatible with studies that have stressed
the lack of difference among business sectors in contributions to
congressional campaigns in the 1970s and 1980s (Clawson, Neustadtl, and Bearden 1986; Burris 1987; Neustadtl and Clawson
1988; Salt 1989; Clawson and Su 1990; Neustadtl, Scott, and
Clawson 1991; Su, Neustadtl, and Clawson 1995). These studies
have demonstrated that there is a high degree of class-based unity
in corporate political contributions, with business giving strong
support to conservative candidates in both the North and South.

Sixth, my findings are supported by studies of voting patterns
that show southern and Jewish voters differentially supported
Democrats in the 1936 presidential election (Campbell, Converse, Millar, and Stokes 1960; Allswang 1978; Ladd and Hadley
1978; Kleppner 1982; Brady 1988; Black and Black 1992; Rae
1994). Religious background is consistently correlated with political behavior—particularly in the years following World War II,
when Catholics and Jews were remarkably Democratic in their
voting patterns and political attitudes across all income levels

(Hamilton 1972:216–17). Southerners, too, continued to be loyal Democratic supporters for many years after the New Deal.

Although the empirical findings of this study are compatible with research on voting behavior and the political history of the New Deal, they also demonstrate the theoretical relevance of a class-dominance perspective. Such a perspective argues that it is possible to recognize the dominance of the power elite without calling its power absolute or uncontested. Rival class segments within the power elite (those fractions of the capitalist class that have a "distinct location in the process of production" [Zeitlin, Neuman, and Radcliff 1976:1009]) may have an overriding interest in maintaining the conditions of capital accumulation, but the mutual rivalry between different class segments seeking to secure their own economic advantage can have a major influence on the policies and actions of the state. One of the key mechanisms by which class segments attempt to exercise such political hegemony is by the formal participation of its representatives in democratic governance—particularly in the leadership of major political parties. In 1936, both the national and international segments of the capitalist class were using the Republican Party as the vehicle for the realization of their political objectives.

Although I have argued that the Democratic Party was controlled by the fringes of the business community (Southerners, small businesses, Catholics, and Jews), it is still capitalist control. This is because the South constituted a distinct class segment within the United States based on an agricultural economy that used both wage labor and capital. Initially founded on slavery, the system later came to depend on the exploitation of its so-called free African American population. Because large landowners occupy a specific class position, they are a distinct class segment within the dominant class, even if industrial capitalism is firmly established in the country as a whole (Zeitlin, Neuman, and Radcliff 1976:1010). The southern segment of the ruling class feared that northern liberals and the federal government would destroy the cultural, political, and economic way of life upon which white southern elite privileges rested. For them, the Democratic Party was a means of influencing state policy and preventing federal intervention in the South. Throughout the 1930s, Roosevelt (recognizing the realities of political power) took care to avoid alienating Southerners on questions of race and labor.

Although the working class may also have distinct class segments, in the United States it has usually been divided by skill, race, and gender rather than segments. During the New Deal years, the severity of the depression, the federal government's support of labor, and the polarization of class antagonisms persuaded many workers to join unions in unprecedented numbers. Although there may be some debate on whether organized labor is a class or whether it represents a class or class segment (Form 1995:7), unionized workers were able to temporarily overcome their differences and exert some pressure on the power elite to make significant changes in American social and economic policy. Following the World War II, labor was in retreat as the Democratic Party increasingly accommodated the demands of Southerners and business interests for anti-union legislation. But these later defeats should not diminish the significance of their alliance with the Democratic Party in the 1930s.

The southern class segment was able to tolerate a complex and uneasy alliance in the Democratic Party with northern liberals (including organized labor, Catholics, Jews, blacks, liberals, progressives, and urban political machines) because they were able to form a prospending alliance around legislation on government management—mainly public works spending—and agricultural assistance—mainly subsidies to big farms (Domhoff 1990:240). This alliance (which emerged during the New Deal) broke down in the 1970s when disagreements over civil rights, social welfare, and the control of organized labor became central political concerns. Up until that time, the southern class segment was able to place real restrictions on liberal and working class initiatives because its dominant position within the Democratic Party gave them effective institutional control of Congress.

Despite the control of both parties by segments of the dominant class, legislation favorable to labor—especially the National Industrial Relations Act of 1935—was passed. This was because of the militancy of the liberal-labor coalition within the Democratic Party and the desertion of northern capitalists by their southern counterparts once liberals offered to exclude seasonal, domestic, and agricultural labor from the legislation (Domhoff 1990:101–4).

From late 1934 to early 1936, Roosevelt was caught between rising working class anger over the failure to enforce the right to organize, and business outrage that strikes were allowed to proceed without state intervention to end them. This became patently obvious during the sit-down in the auto plants of Flint, Michigan, when neither Roosevelt nor Governor Murphy were willing to use coercion against the strikers (Fine 1965; Bernstein 1970). As Piven and Cloward have argued, "the polarizing impact of the labor movement forced Roosevelt's hand" and also helped shape the New Deal coalition that was emerging from the interaction between social movements and electoral politics (1997:294). Organized labor (in conjunction with other liberal groups) was able to work within the Democratic Party to effect lasting changes to the political and economic system.

Thus, a class-dominance perspective that is sensitive to religion and region, as well as the broader contours of social conflict that are produced by rival classes and class segments, has enormous explanatory potential for the 1930s—especially when compared to other theories of the state. It recognizes that the capitalist class is an active and dominant political actor, but argues that in a formally democratic polity it must mobilize in an effective way to prevent other social groups from having the kind of access to state power that may change the conditions of capital accumulation.

Furthermore, class-dominance theory acknowledges that different policies may benefit different capitalists at different times—in other words, the capitalist class itself is not always unified, singular, and monolithic but is often diverse, plural, and fragmented. It is in this context that political mobilization by grassroots movements and other social groups can open up possibilities for change. Although capitalists may support different policies at different times, they do so with varying degrees of enthusiasm and are always less supportive of liberal policies than they are of conservative ones. This is because liberal policies involve a transfer of resources, power, and legitimacy from capitalists to other groups and because of the general distrust American capitalists have for the state (Himmelstein 1990:161–64).

Contemporary political analyses (especially of the Democratic

Party) have tended to focus on arguments that highlight the actions of key political and business elites as being the crucial factor
that determines political outcomes. This view not only considers
grassroots political activism as largely irrelevant to the conduct of
American politics, but it also argues that the Democrats must
move to the right and into the suburbs if they are to become
the majority party once again. With the electorate already skewed
towards the affluent, educated, white voter, such demands would
only further disenfranchise and isolate large groups of poor, minority, and working-class voters.

If there is a lesson to be learned from the New Deal, it is that
the Democratic Party successfully mobilized groups outside the
mainstream of the American power structure to bring about far-
reaching changes in how government responded to the needs of
the American people. It was one of those rare occasions when the
American political system was at least partially responsive to the
demands of ordinary citizens. Social change occurred because
conflict between rival class segments and liberal-labor militancy
coalesced at the same time, creating a window of opportunity for
groups previously marginalized by the American power structure
to bring about reform. By occupying a pivotal place in the Democratic Party, the liberal-labor coalition was able to exploit differences within the dominant class to push reforms through that
benefited many disadvantaged Americans.

Given the structure of the American political system, with its
strong bias against third parties, it is only through capturing control of the Democratic Party that marginalized groups can hope
to have any impact on a government dominated by a capitalist
class that is more concerned with controlling labor markets than
with the plight of the economically and politically disenfranchised. This strategy has been largely ignored by the many leftists
who prefer either to wait for a massive collective movement that
will overthrow capitalism or try to start yet another in a long string
of third parties. But as the "new world order" becomes more
economically and politically fragmented, so an attempt to trans-
form the Democratic Party may provide real opportunities for social change that would be foolish to ignore. In this regard, the
conflicts and struggles of the New Deal era may have much to
teach us about our own time.

METHODOLOGICAL APPENDIX

CAMPAIGN FINANCE DATA FOR THE 1936 PRESIDENTIAL ELECTION

The Federal Corrupt Practices Act of 1925 established the rules and regulations governing the reporting of campaign finance contributions, and these regulations were in effect at the time of the 1936 presidential election. The act required national political committees to have a chairman and treasurer, with the latter being responsible for keeping detailed accounts of the names, addresses, dates, and amounts of the contributions. Furthermore, section 305(a) of the act required treasurers to file information on all contributions of more than $100 with the clerk of the House of Representatives at regular periods throughout the election year (beginning on March 1), with more comprehensive reports submitted on January 1 of each year. According to Louise Overacker (1937:474) (the academic expert on campaign finance for that era), the reports were complete and accurate—especially for the Democrats.

As part of her extensive research on campaign finance for the years between 1928 and 1944, Overacker (1933, 1937, 1941, 1945, 1946) used three-by-five-inch cards to record the information provided to the House of Representatives on donors of $100 or more for the 1936 presidential campaign. She systematically organized the names of contributors that had been randomly entered on legal-size sheets—a task involving a tremendous expenditure of time and energy. Her records are now in the possession of the Citizens Research Foundation at the University of Southern California. Professor Herbert Alexander kindly made these records available to me and they provide the primary database for this analysis because, at the time of writing, they remain the only organized source for 1936 campaign finance data. I am attempting to computerize all the campaign finance data for 1936, however, and in the future, records for other New Deal elections will also be included.

Although the Federal Corrupt Practices Act of 1925 authorized the destruction of the original reports, they are still in existence at the National Archives in Washington, D.C. Detailed information on these records is included in the bibliography (National Archives 1936). It was, therefore, possible to check the accuracy of Overacker's records by drawing a random sample of 100 names from her data and checking it against the original reports. Because there was a perfect match between Overacker's records and the original reports, I have great confidence in the quality of Overacker's archival information and the accuracy of her reporting.

Additional campaign finance data (particularly on wealthy contributors who gave more than $500) came, in part, from the *U.S. Senate Special Committee to Investigate Campaign Contributions for 1937* (hereinafter referred to as the Lonergan Committee). This committee was appointed by the President of the Senate, John N. Garner, on April 14, 1936, to investigate campaign contributions to presidential, vice presidential, and senatorial candidates. The committee was chaired by Augustine Lonergan, a Connecticut Democrat. A freshman senator in 1932, Lonergan gradually became an opponent of the New Deal because of its attack on public utilities, Roosevelt's court-packing plan, and executive reorganization. He was the only conservative Democrat not to be reelected in 1938 (Patterson 1967:288). The other Democrats on the committee were staunch New Dealers: Sherman Minton of Indiana and Lewis B. Schwellenbach of Washington. For the Republicans, conservative Warren V. Austin of Vermont and progressive Robert La Follette of Wisconsin served on the committee. La Follette resigned in September 1936 because of his chairmanship of the Progressive Party and was replaced by the progressive, but isolationist Lynn J. Frazier of North Dakota.

The founding resolution of the committee gave it broad investigative authority to examine campaign contributions to the presidential and senatorial candidates of both parties. It gathered information on the persons, firms, and corporations contributing to these elections. It was also charged with investigating irregularities in campaign finance. Because of the large amount of information collected by the committee, its activities were extended from January to March of 1937.

The Lonergan Committee obtained duplicates of the reports that party organizations had filed with the Clerk of the House of Representatives under the Federal Corrupt Practices Act, along with information directly provided by the national organizations. In addition to this, the committee mailed a questionnaire to the 3,240 people who had contributed more than $500, requesting more specific details about their political contributions. The information obtained from the 62.1 percent who responded was included in the committee's final report. At the end of their deliberations, the Lonergan Committee contended that they had, "conducted a vigorous study into statistics surrounding campaign receipts and contributions in each state, the methods and purposes of such contributions, the number of persons contributing within various ranges, and a special study of all contributions by persons who gave over $500 or more individually to any political organization" (U.S. Congress, Senate 1937:9).

Although the Lonergan Committee had access to records of all who gave more than $100, its report only lists the names of contributors who gave more than $500. Thus, the report is a reliable source for the largest contributors to the 1936 presidential election campaign and it provides further verification of Overacker's record keeping. It records the contributors' names, addresses, and details of the amounts given to the national committees of the major parties, as well as any state or auxiliary organizations. In this study, we used only the contributions of those who gave to the national committees.

Methodological Procedures

A number of strict criteria were established concerning who was to be included as a campaign contributor. First, all company and institutional contributions were excluded so that only individual contributions were included in the final compilation. Second, in noting the party affiliation of Democratic donors, Overacker, in some cases, indicated that the money had been contributed at one of the many fund-raising dinners held regularly by the Democrats in 1936. Because these functions were explicitly political (organized by the Democratic National Committee for the express purpose of raising campaign funds), they were included in the Democratic column. Third, only contributions made between November 1934 and November 1936 were included. Any contributions made before this period could have been intended for the midterm elections of that year; any contributions given after this period could be interpreted as being an attempt to gain access to the vicorious Democrats. In fact, most contributions were given in late 1935 and 1936.

As Thomas Ferguson has pointed out in a critique of my previous work (see Webber 1991; Webber and Domhoff 1996; Ferguson 1995:203–40), not all campaign proceeds in 1936 came from individual donations to the candidate or party. For example, some of the Democratic revenues came from bank loans, business advertisements in a souvenir convention book, business and individual purchases of this book, and labor unions. Although much of my focus is on the preferences of individual business leaders making direct donations, the issue of the Democratic Convention Book of 1936 is dealt with in chapter 5 and the contributions of organized labor are examined in chapter 7.

LIMITATIONS OF THE CAMPAIGN FINANCE DATA

When the data sets were initially combined, it was discovered that a number of Republican contributors listed in the Lonergan Committee report did not appear in Overacker's data. There are a number of possible explanations for this omission. First, Overacker may well have included the Republicans listed in the Lonergan Committee report, but nowhere in her published work is there any mention of how she used this data set. Second, while noting the completeness of the reports from the Democratic National Committee, Overacker was highly critical of Republican reporting methods. She claims that their records are "imperfect carbon copies" with "numerous erasures" which made them difficult to read and so only "approximate accuracy" was possible (1937:474). Third, because of reporting errors, some Republicans may simply have been excluded from her analysis. Finally, the

Democratic National Committee report was submitted to the Lonergan Committee on January 1, 1937, as required by statute. But the Republican National Committee submitted two reports—one on January 1, 1937 which covered the campaign period from June 1 to December 31, 1936 and another report on February 2, 1937, which covered the whole of 1936. In a footnote to her 1937 article, Overacker indicates that she may have only used the report from June through December, 1936. If so, she would have missed the campaign contributions made by Republicans in the first six months of the year.

Without knowing if the missing Republican contributors were connected to the business elite, Overacker cannot be accused of a systematic anti-Republican bias. But it is possible that she slightly underestimated the extent of business support for the Republicans in 1936. In this study (because both the Lonergan Committee and Overacker data sets are used) the list of 1936 Republican contributors is relatively complete.

There also might have been some errors made when the data were initially compiled more than fifty years ago. Because all the information was, and still is, on index cards, there are inevitably problems with human error or the idiosyncratic recording procedures of the researchers—but overall, there were surprisingly few errors. Misspelled names and addresses could be double-checked using a number of bibliographical sources, such as *Who's Who in America, Poor's Register of Directors of the United States and Canada,* 1936, and the *New York Times* obituaries. There were very few mistakes in recording the date of contributions and party affiliation. With regard to the dollar amounts of contributions, there were some discrepancies between the Lonergan and Overacker data sets. In these few cases, I used the larger of the two figures. It should also be borne in mind that the focus of this study is identifying the party affiliation of contributors in particular business sectors, not on the amount of the contribution.

Two types of campaign contributions are not included in the final data set. First, any loans made to either party are not included. Second, any illegal or hidden contributions are not in the files—although they might have been important. These may have taken various forms (e.g., generous corporations might have donated transport, buildings, or even personnel to assist in a candidate's campaign). There is, however, no way of assessing the impact of such "contributions." Without data, the existence and extent of such activities becomes mere speculation.

None of these limitations seriously affects the validity of the data used in this study. The data can be used with considerable confidence to test hypotheses concerning the relation of business to political parties in the New Deal.

BIOGRAPHICAL DATA SOURCES

A significant portion of this study is dedicated to an analysis of the political orientation of corporate officers and directors in various industrial, commercial, and financial sectors to ascertain whether there are any variations in party identification according to economic segment. As with other studies of corporate power, the corporation is used as the unit of analysis. But the embodiment of corporate power is the board of directors, where the dominant actors who initiate and control policy and action within corporate institutions are located.

Moody's Manual of Investments proved to be a valuable source for this study. It is divided into four volumes covering industrials, public utilities, and railroads and one volume for banks, insurance, real estate, and investment trusts. These volumes recorded information on American corporations up to December 1936. Any foreign corporations (including Canadian ones) were excluded from this study. In addition to providing complete and accurate lists of directors according to company, the volumes also categorize firms according to industrial classification and this division was used to place the various corporations in particular economic segments. *Moody's* not only provided the lists of directors, but also gave information on the size of the company (using the company's value according to the balance sheets and other financial records), the number of employees, and the location of the company. All of this information was useful in making classifications based on company size and location.

Poor's Register of Directors of the United States and Canada, 1936, was another important source. With its comprehensive listing of company directors, arranged alphabetically, it gives both the business and residence addresses of the directors, as well as a list of their directorships. This was an invaluable tool for checking the full names and company affiliations of directors who might only have their initials or a misspelled name in the campaign finance data. It increased the validity of the study by ensuring that each director had been matched with the right campaign finance contribution.

The other sources used in this study were biographical sources such as *Who's Who in America, 1930–31* and *1936–37, Who's Who in American Jewry, 1937, Who's Who in New York, 1937,* and the *Italian-American Who's Who, 1937.* The details on how these sources were used are included in the appropriate sections. Also, *The New York Times* (between January 1 and November 7, 1936) was used to provide additional information on political and economic events.

REFERENCES

Adamany, David W. 1972. *Campaign Finance in America*. North Scituate, Mass.: Duxbury Press.

Alexander, Herbert. 1971. Financing Presidential Campaigns. In *History of American Presidential Elections, 1789–1968*, ed. Arthur Schlesinger and Fred L. Israel. New York: Chelsea House Publishers.

———. 1972. *Money in Politics*. Washington, D.C.: Public Affairs Press.

———. 1976. *Financing Politics: Money, Elections, and Political Reform*. 3d ed. Washington, D.C.: Congressional Quarterly Press.

Alford, Robert R., and Roger Friedland. 1985. *Powers of Theory: Capitalism, the State, and Democracy*. Cambridge: Cambridge University Press.

Allen, Michael Patrick. 1987. *The Founding Fortunes*. New York: Truman Talley Books.

———. 1991. "Capitalist Response to State Intervention: Theories of the State and Political Finance in the New Deal." *American Sociological Review* 56(October):679–89.

Allen, Michael Patrick, and Philip Broyles. 1989. "Class Hegemony and Political Finance: Presidential Campaign Contributions of Wealthy Capitalist Families." *American Sociological Review* 54(April):275–87.

Allswang, John. 1978. *The New Deal and American Politics*. New York: John Wiley and Sons.

Almond, Gabriel. 1998. *Plutocracy and Politics in New York City*. Boulder: Westview Press.

Amalgamated Clothing Workers of America. 1926. *Report of the General Executive Board and Proceedings of the Seventh Biennial Convention of the Amalgamated Clothing Workers of America*. Montréal: Amalgamated Clothing Workers of America, 1926.

American Catholic Who's Who, 1936 and *1937*. 2d ed. Detroit: Walter Romig and Co.

Badger, Anthony. 1989. *The New Deal: The Depression Years, 1933–1940.* New York: The Noonday Press.

Baltzell, E. Digby. 1958. *Philadelphia Gentlemen: The Making of a National Upper Class.* Glencoe, Ill.: Free Press.

———. 1964. *The Protestant Establishment.* New York: Random House.

———. 1966. Who's Who in America and the Social Register: Elite and Upper Class Indexes in Metropolitan America. In *Class, Status, and Power: Social Stratification in Contemporary Perspective,* ed. Reinhart Benedix and Seymour Martin Lipset. New York: Free Press.

Banfield, Edward C., and James Q. Wilson. 1967. *City Politics.* Cambridge: Harvard University Press.

Barrows, Clyde W. 1993. *Critical Theories of the State.* Madison: University of Wisconsin Press.

Bartley, Numan V., and Hugh D. Graham. 1975. *Southern Politics and the Second Reconstruction.* Baltimore: Johns Hopkins University Press.

Bayor, Ronald H. 1988. *Neighbors in Conflict: The Irish, Germans, Jews, and Italians of New York City, 1929–1941.* 2d ed. Urbana: University of Illinois Press.

Beatty, Jack. 1995. "The Road to a Third Party." *Atlantic Monthly* August: 101–4.

Benson, Lee. 1961. *The Concept of Jacksonian Democracy.* Princeton: Princeton University Press.

Berger, Mark L. 1995. "Franklin D. Roosevelt and Cason J. Callaway: An Enduring Friendship." *Georgia Historical Quarterly* 79(winter):904–19.

Bernstein, Irving. 1970. *Turbulent Years: A History of the American Worker, 1933–1941.* Boston: Houghton Mifflin.

Biles, Roger. 1994. *The South and the New Deal.* Lexington: University of Kentucky Press.

Black, Earl, and Merle Black. 1987. *Politics and Society in the South.* Cambridge: Harvard University Press.

———. 1992. *The Vital South: How Presidents Are Elected.* Cambridge: Harvard University Press.

Blocker, Jack S., Jr. 1989. *American Temperance Movements: Cycles of Reform.* Boston: Twayne Publishers.

Bohrnstedt, George, and David Knoke. 1994. *Statistics for Social Data Analysis*. 3d ed. Itasca, Ill.: F. E. Peacock.

Brady, David W. 1988. *Critical Elections and Congressional Policy Making*. Stanford: Stanford University Press.

Brody, David. 1985. "The CIO after 50 Years." *Dissent* 32 (fall): 457–72.

Brown, Clifford W., Jr., Linda W. Powell, and Clyde Wilcox. 1995. *Serious Money: Fundraising and Contributing in Presidential Nominating Campaigns*. Cambridge: Cambridge University Press.

Brustein, William. 1989. *The Social Origins of Political Regionalism in France, 1849–1981*. Berkeley: University of California Press.

Burk, Robert F. 1990. *The Corporate State and the Broker State*. Cambridge: Harvard University Press.

Burner, David. 1968. *The Politics of Provincialism: The Democratic Party in Transition, 1918–1932*. New York: Alfred A. Knopf.

Burnham, Walter Dean. 1970. *Critical Elections and the Mainsprings of American Politics*. New York: W. W. Norton.

Burris, Val. 1987. "The Political Partisanship of American Business." *American Sociological Review* 52 (December):732–44.

Callow, Alexander. 1966. *The Tweed Ring*. New York: Oxford University Press.

Camilli, Gregory. 1995. "The relationship between Fisher's exact test and Pearson's chi-square test: A Bayesian perspective." *Psychometrika* 60 (June):305–12.

Camilli, Gregory, and Kenneth D. Hopkins. 1978. "Applicability of chi-square to 2x2 contingency tables with small expected cell frequencies." *Psychological Bulletin* 85 (January):163–67.

Camilli, Gregory, and Kenneth D. Hopkins. 1979. "Testing for association in 2x2 contingency tables with very small sample sizes." *Psychological Bulletin* 86 (September):1011–14.

Cammack, Paul. 1989. "Review Article: Bringing the State Back In?" *British Journal of Political Science* 19 (April):261–90.

Campbell, Angus, Philip E. Converse, William E. Millar, and Donald E. Stokes. 1960. *The American Voter*. New York: John Wiley and Sons.

Carnoy, Martin. 1984. *The State and Political Theory*. Princeton: Princeton University Press.

Carosso, Vincent P. 1970. *Investment Banking in America*. Cambridge: Harvard University Press.

Cash, Wilbur J. 1941. *The Mind of the South*. New York: Alfred A. Knopf.

Clawson, Dan, Alan Neustadtl, and Denise Scott. 1992. *Money Talks: Corporate PACs and Political Influence*. New York: Basic Books.

Clawson, Dan, Alan Neustadtl, and Mark Weller. 1998. *Dollars and Votes: How Business Campaign Contributions Subvert Democracy*. Philadelphia: Temple University Press.

Clawson, Dan, and Tie-ting Su. 1990. "Was 1980 Special? A Comparison of 1980 and 1986 Corporate PAC Contributions." *Sociological Quarterly* 31 (summer):371–87.

Clawson, Dan, Alan Neustadtl, and James Bearden. 1986. "The Logic of Business Unity: Corporate Contributions to the 1980 Congressional Elections." *American Sociological Review* 51 (December):797–811.

Clubb, Jerome M., William H. Flanigan, and Nancy H. Zingale. 1990. *Partisan Realignment: Voters, Parties, and Government in American History*. Boulder: Westview Press.

Cobb, James. 1988. "Beyond Planters and Industrialists: A New Perspective on the American South." *Journal of Southern History* 54(1):45–68.

Cohen, Lizabeth. 1990. *Making a New Deal: Industrial Workers in Chicago, 1919–1939*. Cambridge: Cambridge University Press.

Cohen, Steven. 1989. *The Dimensions of American Jewish Liberalism*. New York: American Jewish Committee.

Corrado, Anthony. 1992. *Creative Campaigning: PAC's and the Presidential Selection Process*. Boulder: Westview Press.

Dahl, Robert A. 1961. *Who Governs? Democracy and Power in an American City*. New Haven: Yale University Press.

Danish, Max D. 1957. *The World of David Dubinsky*. New York: World Publishing Company.

Degler, Carl N. 1959. *Out of Our Past: The Forces that Shaped Modern America*. 1st ed. New York: Harper and Row.

Domhoff, G. William. 1972. *Fat Cats and Democrats*. Englewood Cliffs, N.J.: Prentice-Hall.

———. 1987. "Corporate Liberal Theory and the Social Security Act: A Chapter in the Sociology of Knowledge." *Politics and Society* 15(3):297–330.

————. 1990. *The Power Elite and the State*. Hawthorne, N.Y.: Aldine de Gruyter.

————. 1996. *State Autonomy or Class Dominance? Case Studies on Policy Making in America*. Hawthorne, N.Y.: Aldine de Gruyter.

————. 1998. *Who Rules America? Power and Politics in the Year 2000*. Mountain View, Calif.: Mayfield Publishing.

Dorsett, Lyle W. 1977. *Franklin D. Roosevelt and the City Bosses*. Port Washington, N.Y.: Kennikat Press.

Dubofsky, Melvyn, and Warren Van Tine. 1987. John L. Lewis and the Triumph of Mass Production Unionism. In *Labor Leaders in America*, ed. Melvyn Dubofsky and Warren Van Tine. Urbana: University of Illinois Press.

Dulles, Foster Rhea, and Melvyn Dubofsky. 1984. *Labor in America: A History*. 4th ed. Arlington Heights, Ill.: Harlan Davidson.

Eldersveld, Samuel J. 1949. "The Influence of Metropolitan Party Pluralities in Presidential Elections Since 1920: A Study of Twelve Key Cities." *American Political Science Review* 43(December):1189–209.

Epstein, Melech. 1969. *Jewish Labor in America: An Industrial, Political, and Cultural History of the Jewish Labor Movement, 1882–1914*. New York: Ktav Publishing House.

Erie, Steven P. 1988. *Rainbow's End: Irish-Americans and the Dilemmas of Urban Machine Politics, 1840–1985*. Berkeley: University of California Press.

Ferguson, George. 1981. *Statistical Analysis in Psychology and Education*. 5th ed. New York: McGraw-Hill.

Ferguson, Thomas 1984. "From Normalcy to New Deal: Industrial Structure, Party Competition and American Public Policy in the Great Depression." *International Organization* 38(winter):41–92.

————. 1995. *Golden Rule: The Investment Theory of Party Competition and the Logic of Money-Driven Political Systems*. Chicago: University of Chicago Press.

Fine, Sidney. 1965. *Sitdown: The General Motors Strike of 1936–1937*. Ann Arbor: University of Michigan Press.

Finegold, Kenneth, and Theda Skocpol. 1995. *State and Party in America's New Deal*. Madison: University of Wisconsin Press.

Flynn, George Q. 1968. *American Catholics and the Roosevelt Presidency, 1932–1936*. Lexington: University of Kentucky Press.

Forbath, William E. 1991. *Law and The Shaping of the American Labor Movement*. Cambridge: Harvard University Press.

Form, William. 1995. *Segmented Labor, Fractured Politics: Labor Politics in American Life*. New York: Plenum Press.

Fraser, Steven. 1984. "From the 'New Unionism' to the New Deal." *Labor History* 25(summer):422–33.

———. 1989. "The Labor Question" In *The Rise and Fall of the New Deal Order, 1930–1980*, ed. Steve Fraser and Gary Gerstle. Princeton: Princeton University Press.

———. 1991. *Labor Will Rule: Sidney Hillman and the Rise of American Labor*. New York: Free Press.

Friedlander, Peter. 1987. "The Origins of the Welfare State: The Keynesian Elite and the Second New Deal." Manuscript. Detroit: Wayne State University.

Fuchs, Lawrence. 1956. *The Political Behavior of American Jews*. Glencoe, Ill.: The Free Press.

———, ed. 1968. *American Ethnic Politics*. New York: Harper and Row.

Gais, Thomas. 1996. *Improper Influence: Campaign Finance Law, Political Interest Groups, and the Problem of Equality*. Ann Arbor: University of Michigan Press.

Galambos, Louis. 1966. *Competition and Cooperation: The Emergence of a National Trade Association*. Baltimore: Johns Hopkins University Press.

Gallup, George, Jr., and Jim Castelli. 1987. *The American Catholic People*. Garden City, N.J.: Doubleday.

Garrett, Charles. 1961. *The La Guardia Years: Machine and Reform Politics in New York City*. New Brunswick, N.J.: Rutgers University Press.

Gilbert, Jess, and Carolyn Howe. 1991. "Beyond 'State vs Society': Theories of the State and New Deal Agricultural Policy." *American Sociological Review* 56(April):201–20.

Ginsberg, Benjamin. 1993. *The Fatal Embrace: Jews and the State*. Chicago: University of Chicago Press.

Goldfield, Michael. 1989. "Worker Insurgency, Radical Organization, and New Deal Labor Legislation." *American Political Science Review* 83(December):1257–82.

Gordon, Colin. 1994. *New Deals: Business, Labor, and Politics in America, 1920–1935*. Cambridge: Cambridge University Press.

Gosnell, Harold F. 1937. *Machine Politics: Chicago Model.* Chicago: University of Chicago Press.

———. 1952. *Champion Campaigner.* New York: Macmillan.

Gourevitch, Peter. 1985. "Breaking with Orthodoxy: The Politics of Economic Policy Response to the Depression of the 1930s." *International Organization* 38(winter):95–126.

Grantham, Dewey. 1994. *The South in Modern America: A Region at Odds.* New York: Harper Collins Publishers.

Greenstone, J. David. 1969. *Labor in American Politics.* New York: Alfred A. Knopf.

Hamilton, Richard. 1972. *Class and Politics in the United States.* New York: John Wiley and Sons.

———. 1996. *The Social Misconstruction of Reality.* New Haven: Yale University Press.

Harris, Leon. 1977. *Merchant Princes: An Intimate History of Jewish Families Who Built Great Department Stores.* New York: Harper and Row.

Hattam, Victoria C. 1993. *Labor Visions and State Power: The Origins of Business Unionism in the United States.* Princeton: Princeton University Press.

Hawley, Ellis. 1966. *The New Deal and the Problem of Monopoly: A Study in Economic Ambivalence.* Princeton: Princeton University Press.

Heard, Alexander. 1962. *The Costs of Democracy.* New York: Anchor Books.

Held, David. 1984. *Political Theory and the Modern State.* Palo Alto, Calif.: Stanford University Press.

Himmelfarb, Harold S., Michael Loar, and Susan Mott. 1983. "Sampling by Ethnic Surnames: The Case of American Jews." *Public Opinion Quarterly* 47(summer):247–60.

Himmelstein, Jerome L. 1990. *To the Right: The Transformation of American Conservatism.* Berkeley: University of California Press.

Hodges, James A. 1986. *New Deal Labor Policy and the Southern Cotton Textile Industry, 1933–1941.* Knoxville: The University of Tennessee Press.

Hooks, Gregory. 1990. "From an Autonomous to a Captured State Agency: The Decline of the New Deal in Agriculture." *American Sociological Review* 55(February):29–43.

Isaacs, Stephen D. 1974. *Jews and American Politics.* Garden City, N.Y.: Doubleday and Co.

Italian-American Who's Who, a Biographical Dictionary of Italian-American Leaders and Distinguished Italian Residents of the United States.

Jenkins, J. Craig, and Barbara Brents. 1989. "Social Protest, Hegemonic Competition, and Social Reform: A Political Struggle Interpretation of the American Welfare State." *American Sociological Review* 54(December):891–909.

Jensen, Richard J. 1971. *The Winning of the Midwest: Social and Political Conflict, 1888–1896.* Chicago: University of Chicago Press.

Jessop, Bob. 1990. *State Theory.* University Park: Pennsylvania State University Press.

Jones, Jacqueline. 1998. *American Work: Four Centuries of Black and White Labor.* New York: W. W. Norton and Co.

Katznelson, Ira. 1981. *City Trenches: Urban Politics and the Patterning of Class in the United States.* New York: Pantheon Books.

Kennedy, John. 1992. *Analyzing Qualitative Data.* 2d ed. New York: Praeger Press.

Kerr, K. Austin. 1985. *Organized for Prohibition: A New History of the Anti-Saloon League.* New Haven: Yale University Press.

Kessner, Thomas. 1989. *Fiorello H. La Guardia and the Making of Modern New York.* New York: McGraw-Hill Publishing Co.

Key, V.O. 1955. "A Theory of Critical Elections." *Journal of Politics* 17(February):3–18.

———. 1984. *Southern Politics in State and Nation.* New Edition. Knoxville: University of Tennessee Press.

Kleppner, Paul. 1970. *The Cross of Culture: A Social Analysis of Midwestern Politics, 1850–1900.* New York: Greenwood Press.

———. 1979. *The Third Electoral System, 1853–1892: Parties, Voters, and Political Cultures.* Chapel Hill: University of North Carolina Press.

———. 1982. *Who Voted? The Dynamics of Electoral Turnout, 1870–1980.* New York: Praeger Publishers.

Knoke, David. 1976. *Change and Continuity in American Politics: The Social Bases of Political Parties.* Baltimore: Johns Hopkins University Press.

Kousser, J. Morgan. 1974. *The Shaping of Southern Politics.* New Haven: Yale University Press.

Kyvig, David E. 1979. *Repealing National Prohibition.* Chicago: University of Chicago Press.

———. 1985. Sober Thoughts, Myths and Realities of National Prohibition after Fifty Years. In *Law, Alcohol, and Order: Perspectives on National Prohibition,* ed. David E. Kyvig. Westport, Conn.: Greenwood Press.

Ladd, Everett Carl, with Charles D. Hadley. 1978. *Transformations of the American Party System.* 2d ed. New York: W. W. Norton and Co.

Laumann, Edward O., and David R. Siegal. 1971. "Status Inconsistency and Ethnoreligious Group Membership as Determinants of Social Participation and Political Attitudes." *American Journal of Sociology* 77 (July):36–61.

Lazerwitz, Bernard 1986. "Some Comments on the Use of Distinctive Jewish Names in Surveys." *Contemporary Jewry* 7:85–91.

Leff, Mark. 1981. *The Limits of Symbolic Reform: The New Deal and Taxation, 1933–1939.* Cambridge: Cambridge University Press.

Leuchtenburg, William E. 1963. *Franklin D. Roosevelt and the New Deal, 1932–1940.* New York: Harper and Row.

———. 1995. *The FDR Years.* New York: Columbia University Press.

Levine, Rhonda. 1988. *Class Struggle and the New Deal: Industrial Labor, Industrial Capital, and the State.* Lawrence: University Press of Kansas.

Levy, Mark R., and Michael S. Kramer. 1972. *The Ethnic Factor: How America's Minorities Decide Elections.* New York: Simon and Schuster.

Lichtenstein, Nelson. 1989. From Corporatism to Collective Bargaining: Organized Labor and the Eclipse of Social Democracy in the Postwar Era. In *The Rise and Fall of the New Deal Order, 1930–1980,* ed. Steve Fraser and Gary Gerstle. Princeton: Princeton University Press.

Lichtman, Allan J. 1979. *Prejudice and the Old Politics.* Chapel Hill: University of North Carolina Press.

Lieberson, Stanley, and Donna Carter. 1979. "Making it in America: Differences Between Eminent Blacks and White Ethnic Groups." *American Sociological Review* 44 (June):347–66.

Lindblom, Charles E. 1977. *Politics and Markets: The World's Political Economic Systems.* New York: Basic Books.

Lipset, Seymour Martin. 1968. *Revolution and Counter Revolution: Change and Persistence in Social Structures.* New York: Basic Books.

Lipset, Seymour Martin, and Earl Raab. 1995. *Jews and the New American Scene.* Cambridge: Harvard University Press.

Logan, John and Harvey Molotch. 1987. *Urban Fortunes.* Berkeley: University of California Press.

Lowi, Theodore. 1964. *At the Pleasure of the Mayor: Patronage and Power in New York City, 1898–1958.* New York: Free Press.

Lundberg, Ferdinand. 1937. *America's Sixty Families.* New York: Vanguard Press.

Mandelbaum, Seymour. 1965. *Boss Tweed's New York.* New York: John Wiley and Sons.

Martin, Boyce F. 1941. "Southern Industrial Development." *Harvard Business Review* 19(winter):162–76.

Mayer, William G. 1996. *The Divided Democrats: Ideological Unity, Party Reform, and Presidential Elections.* Boulder: Westview Press.

McCormick, Richard L. 1986. *The Party Period and Public Policy: American Politics from the Age of Jackson to the Progressive Era.* New York: Oxford University Press.

Mettler, Suzanne. 1998. *Dividing Citizens: Gender and Federalism in New Deal Public Policy.* Ithaca, N.Y.: Cornell University Press.

Michelson, Charles. 1944. *The Ghost Talks.* New York: G. P. Putnam's Sons.

Mills, C. Wright. 1956. *The Power Elite.* New York: Oxford University Press.

————. 1979. The Trade Union Leader: A Collective Portrait. In *Power, Politics, and People: The Collected Essays of C. Wright Mills,* ed. Irving L. Horowitz. New York: Oxford University Press.

Mintz, Beth, and Michael Schwartz. 1985. *The Power Structure of American Business.* Chicago: University of Chicago Press.

Mitchell, Timothy. 1991. "The Limits of the State: Beyond Statist Approaches and Their Critics." *American Political Science Review* 85(March):77–96.

Mizruchi, Mark S. 1992. *The Structure of Corporate Political Action: Interfirm Relations and their Consequences.* Cambridge: Harvard University Press.

Moody's Manual of Investments: Banks, Insurance, Real Estate and Trusts. 1937. New York: Moody's Investment Service.

Moody's Manual of Investments: Industrial Securities. 1937. New York: Moody's Investment Service.

Moore, Deborah. 1981. *At Home in America: Second Generation New York Jews.* New York: Columbia University Press.

Mushkat, Jerome. 1971. *Tammany.* Syracuse: Syracuse University Press.

Nardulli, Peter F. 1995. "The Concept of a Critical Realignment, Electoral Behavior, and Political Change." *American Political Science Review* 89 (March):10–22.

National Archives. 1936. Records of the U.S. House of Representatives (1936 Presidential Campaign). Record Group 233: "Democratic National Committee (Receipts) January 1, 1936–December 31, 1936." Vol. 50; "Democratic Miscellaneous Reports." Vol. 53; "Reports No. 645–1039" Vol. 54; "Republican National Committee Receipts and Disbursements January 1936–August 31 1936" Vol. 56; "Republican National Committee Contributions September 1, 1936–December 31, 1936" Vol. 57.

Neustadtl, Alan, and Dan Clawson. 1988. "Corporate Political Groupings: Does Ideology Unify Business Political Behavior?" *American Sociological Review* 53 (April):172–90.

Neustadtl, Alan, Denise Scott, and Dan Clawson. 1991. "Class Struggle in Campaign Finance? Political Action Committee Contributions in the 1984 Elections." *Sociological Forum* 6 (June):219–38.

New York Times. 1936a. "Jesse Straus Dies of Pneumonia Here." 5 October, 1:4

———. 1936b. "Farley To Sell a Fancy Program." 5 April, 43:1

———. 1936c. "Republican Outlay $4,000,000 To Date." 20 October, 1:3

———. 1942. "L. E. Kirstein Dies: Boston Merchant." 11 December, 23:1

———. 1944. "Percy Straus, 67, Dies in Home Here." 8 April, 13:1

———. 1953. "Herman B. Baruch, Former U.S. Envoy." 16 March, 19:4

———. 1959. "George H. Johnson Dies at 74: Hotel President in Philadelphia." 14 October, 43:2

————. 1962. "John J. Turtletaub, Real Estate Man, 68." 10 May, 37:2

————. 1966. "Bernard F. Gimbel Dies at 81: Led Chain of Stores 34 Years." 30 September, 1:5

————. 1967. "Albert M. Greenfield Dies at 79: Built Realty and Store Empire." 6 January, 35:1

Nie, Norman, Sidney Verba, and John R. Petrocik. 1979. *The Changing American Voter.* Cambridge: Harvard University Press.

Noble, Charles. 1987. Review of *Right Turn: The Decline of the Democrats and the Future of American Politics,* by Thomas Ferguson and Joel Rodgers. *American Political Science Review* 81(September):993–94.

Ortiz, Altagracia. 1990. Puerto Ricans in the Garment Industry of New York City, 1920–1960. In *Labor Divided: Race and Ethnicity in United States Labor Struggles, 1835–1960,* ed. Robert Asher and Charles Stephenson. Albany: SUNY Press.

Overacker, Louise. 1932. *Money in Elections.* New York: Macmillan Co.

————. 1933. "Campaign Funds in a Depression Year." *American Political Science Review* 27(October):769–83.

————. 1937. "Campaign Funds in the Presidential Election of 1936." *American Political Science Review* 31(June):473–98.

————. 1939. "Labor's Political Contributions." *Political Science Quarterly* 14(March):56–68.

————. 1941. "Campaign Finance in the Presidential Election of 1940." *American Political Science Review* 35(August):701–27.

————. 1945. "Presidential Campaign Funds, 1944." *American Political Science Review* 39(October):899–925.

————. 1946. *Presidential Campaign Funds.* Boston: Boston University Press.

Parrish, Michael E. 1992. *Anxious Decades: America in Prosperity and Depression, 1920–1941.* New York: W. W. Norton.

Patterson, James T. 1967. *Congressional Conservatism and the New Deal.* Westport, Conn.: Greenwood Publishers.

————. 1969. *The New Deal and the States: Federalism in Transition.* Princeton: Princeton University Press.

Piven, Francis Fox, and Richard Cloward. 1997. *The Breaking of the American Compact.* New York: New Press.

Plotke, David. 1996. *Building a Democratic Political Order: Reshaping*

American Liberalism in the 1930s and 1940s. Cambridge: Cambridge University Press.

Pollock, James. 1926. *Party Campaign Funds.* New York: Alfred A. Knopf.

Poor's Register of Directors of the United States and Canada, Geographical Section. 1936. New York: Poor's Publishing Co.

Poor's Register of Directors of the United States and Canada. 1936. New York: Poor's Publishing Co.

Potter, David M. 1972. *The South and the Concurrent Majority.* Baton Rouge: Louisiana State University Press.

Pound, Arthur. 1935. *The Golden Earth: The Story of Manhattan's Landed Wealth.* New York: Macmillan.

Quadagno, Jill. 1984. "Welfare Capitalism and the Social Security Act of 1935." *American Sociological Review* 49 (October):632–47.

———. 1988. *The Transformation of Old Age Security.* Chicago: University of Chicago Press.

Rae, Nicol C. 1994. *Southern Democrats.* New York: Oxford University Press.

Reynolds, H. J. 1984. *Analysis of Nominal Data.* 2d ed. Newbury Park, Calif.: Sage Publications.

Robinson, Donald B. 1948. *Spotlight on a Union: The Story of the United Hatters, Cap and Millinery Workers International Union.* New York: Dual Press.

Rochester, Anna. 1936. *Rulers of America: A Study of Finance Capital.* New York: International Publishers.

Rose, Arnold M. 1967. *The Power Structure: Political Process in American Society.* New York: Oxford University Press.

Rosen, Eliot. 1977. *Hoover, Roosevelt, and the Brains Trust.* New York: Columbia University Press.

Rosenstone, Steven J., Roy L. Behr, and Edward H. Lazarus. 1984. *Third Parties in America: Citizen Response to Major Party Failure.* Princeton: Princeton University Press.

Rosenthal, Robert, and David Rubin. 1982. "A Simple General Purpose Display of Magnitude of Experimental Effect." *Journal of Educational Psychology* 74 (February):166–69.

Rumbarger, John. 1989. *Profits, Power, and Prohibition: Alcohol Reform and the Industrializing of America, 1800–1930.* Albany: SUNY Press.

Salt, James. 1989. "Sunbelt Capital and Conservative Political Realignment in the 1970s and 1980s." *Critical Sociology* 16 (summer-fall):145–63.

Sabato, Larry. 1989. *Pay for Elections: The Campaign Finance Thicket.* New York: Priority Press.

Sachar, Howard M. 1992. *A History of the Jews in America.* New York: Alfred A. Knopf.

Savage, Sean J. 1991. *Roosevelt the Party Leader, 1932–1945.* Lexington: University Press of Kentucky.

Schlesinger, Arthur. 1958. *The Age of Roosevelt, Vol II: The Coming of the New Deal.* Boston: Houghton Mifflin Co.

———. 1960. *The Age of Roosevelt, Vol III: The Politics of Upheaval.* Boston: Houghton Mifflin Co.

Schulman, Bruce J. 1994. *From Cotton Belt to Sunbelt: Federal Policy, Economic Development, and the Transformation of the South, 1938–1980.* Durham, N.C.: Duke University Press.

Shafer, Byron E., ed. 1991. *The End of Realignment? Interpreting American Electoral Eras.* Madison: University of Wisconsin Press.

Shefter, Martin. 1988. Political Incorporation and Containment: Regime Transformation in New York City. In *Power, Culture, and Place: Essays on New York City,* ed. John Hull Mollenkopf. New York: Russell Sage Foundation.

Shannon, Jasper B. 1948. Presidential Politics in the South. In *The Southern Political Scene, 1938–1948,* ed. Taylor Cole and John H. Hallowell. Gainesville, Fla.: Kallman Publishing Company.

Skocpol, Theda. 1980. "Political Response to Capitalist Crisis: Neo-Marxist Theories of the State and the Case of the New Deal." *Politics and Society* 10(2):155–201.

Skocpol, Theda, and Edwin Amenta. 1985. "Did Capitalists Shape Social Security?" *American Sociological Review* 50(August):572–75.

Skocpol, Theda, and Kenneth Finegold. 1982. "State Capacity and Economic Intervention in the Early New Deal." *Political Science Quarterly* 97(summer):255–78.

Skocpol, Theda, and Kenneth Finegold. 1984. State, Party, and Industry: From Business Recovery to the Wagner Act in the New Deal. In *State Making and Social Movements: Essays in History and Theory,* ed. Charles Bright and Susan Harding. Ann Arbor: University of Michigan Press.

Skocpol, Theda, and Kenneth Finegold. 1990. "Explaining New

Deal Labor Policy." *American Political Science Review* 84 (December):1297–304.

Skocpol, Theda, and John Ikenberry. 1983. "The Political Formation of the American Welfare State in Historical and Comparative Perspective." *Comparative Social Research* 6:87–148.

Smith, Douglas L. 1988. *The New Deal in the Urban South.* Baton Rouge: Louisiana State University Press.

Social Register of New York. 1937. Vol. 51, no. 1. (November). New York: Social Register Association.

Sorauf, Frank J. 1992. *Inside Campaign Finance: Myths and Realities.* New Haven: Yale University Press.

Soule, George. 1939. *Sidney Hillman: Labor Statesman.* New York: Macmillan Press.

Stave, Bruce H. 1970. *The New Deal and the Last Hurrah: Pittsburgh Machine Politics.* Pittsburgh: University of Pittsburgh Press.

Stolberg, Benjamin. 1944. *Taylor's Progress: The Story of a Famous Union and the Men Who Made It.* New York: Doubleday, Doran, and Co.

Stott, Richard. 1989. Hinterland Development and Differences in Work Setting: The New York City Region, 1820–1870. In *New York and the Rise of American Capitalism,* ed. William Pencak and Conrad Edick Wright. New York: New York Historical Society.

Su, Tie-ting, Alan Neustadtl, and Dan Clawson. 1995. "Business and the Conservative Shift: Corporate PAC Contributions, 1976–1980." *Social Science Quarterly* 76 (March):20–40.

Sundquist, James L. 1973. *Dynamics of the Party System: Alignment and Realignment of Political Parties in the United States.* Washington, D.C.: The Brookings Institution.

Swenson, Peter. 1997. "Arranged Alliance: Business Interests in the New Deal." *Politics and Society* 25 (March):66–116.

Swierenga, Robert P. 1990. Ethnoreligious Political Behavior in the Mid-Nineteenth Century: Voting, Values, and Culture. In *Religion and American Politics,* ed. Mark A. Noll. New York: Oxford University Press.

Thayer, George. 1973. *Who Shakes the Money Tree: Presidential Campaign Finance.* New York: Simon and Schuster.

Tindall, George B. 1967. *The Emergence of the New South, 1913–1945.* Baton Rouge: Louisiana State University Press.

Tomlins, Christopher. 1985. *The State and the Unions: Labor Rela-*

tions, Law, and the Organized Labor Movement in America, 1880–1960. Cambridge: Cambridge University Press.

Tolchin, Martin, and Susan Tolchin. 1971. *To the Victor . . .* New York: Random House.

Trout, Charles H. 1977. *Boston: The Great Depression and the New Deal*. New York: Oxford University Press.

Troy, Gil. 1997. "Money and Politics: The Oldest Connection." *Wilson Quarterly* 21 (summer):14–32.

Truman, David B. 1971. *The Governmental Process: Political Interests and Public Opinion*. 2d ed. New York: Alfred P. Knopf.

Tyler, Gus. 1995. *Look for the Union Label: A History of the International Ladies Garment Workers' Union*. New York: M. E. Sharpe.

U.S. Congress. Senate. 1937. *Report of the Special Committee to Investigate Campaign Expenditures of Presidential, Vice-Presidential and Senatorial Candidates in 1936*. 75th Congress, 1st Session, 1936, S. Rept. 151.

———. 1940. *Report of the Special Committee to Investigate Presidential, Vice-Presidential, and Senatorial Campaign Expenditures, 1940*. 77th Congress, 1st Session, 1940, S. Rept. 47.

———. 1944. *Report of the Special Committee to Investigate Presidential, Vice-Presidential, and Senatorial Campaign Expenditures, 1944*. 79th Congress, 1st Session, 1944, S. Rept. 101.

U.S. Bureau of the Census. 1933. *Abstract of the Fifteenth Census of the United States: 1930*. Washington, D.C.: Government Printing Office.

———. 1975. *Historical Statistics of the United States from Colonial Times to 1970*. Washington, D.C.: Bureau of the Census.

U.S. Bureau of Foreign and Domestic Commerce. 1937. *Statistical Abstracts of the United States, 1937*. Washington, D.C.: Government Printing Office.

U.S. National Resources Committee. 1939. *The Structure of the American Economy: Part I. Basic Characteristics*. Washington, D.C.: Government Printing Office.

Useem, Michael. 1984. *The Inner Circle*. New York: Oxford University Press.

van den Berg, Axel. 1988. *The Immanent Utopia: From Marxism on the State to the State of Marxism*. Princeton: Princeton University Press.

Vittoz, Stanley. 1987. *New Deal Labor Policy and the American Industrial Economy.* Chapel Hill: University of North Carolina Press.

Wald, Kenneth D. 1997. *Religion and Politics in the United States.* 3d ed. Washington, D.C.: Congressional Quarterly Press.

Waltzer, Kenneth A. 1977. The American Labor Party: Third Party Politics in New Deal-Cold War New York, 1936–1954. Ph.D diss., Harvard University.

Webber, Michael J. 1991. "Business, the Democratic Party, and the New Deal: An Empirical Critique of Thomas Ferguson's 'Investment Theory of Politics.'" *Sociological Perspectives* 34(winter):473–92.

Webber, Michael J., and G. William Domhoff. 1996. "Myth and Reality in Business Support for Democrats and Republicans in the 1936 Presidential Election." *American Political Science Review* 90(December):824–33.

Weber, Max. 1993. *Basic Concepts in Sociology.* New York: Citadel Press.

Wenger, S. Beth. 1996. *New York Jews and the Great Depression.* New Haven: Yale University Press.

Whitfield, Stephen J. 1986. "The Jewish Vote." *Virginia Quarterly Review* 62(winter):1–20.

Who's Who in America, 1936–37. Volume 19. Chicago: The A. N. Marquis Company.

Who's Who in American Jewry, 1938–39. New York: Jewish Biographical Bureau.

Who's Who in New York (City and State). 1938. 10th ed. New York: Lewis Historical Publishing Company.

Wolfskill, George. 1962. *The Revolt of the Conservatives.* Boston: Houghton Mifflin Company.

Wolfskill, George, and John A. Hudson. 1969. *All But the People: Franklin D. Roosevelt and his Critics, 1933–1939.* London: Macmillan.

Zeitlin, Maurice, W. Lawrence Neuman, and Richard R. Radcliff. 1976. "Class Segments: Agrarian Property and Political Leadership in the Capitalist Class of Chile." *American Sociological Review* 41(December):1006–29.

Zieger, Robert H. 1994. *American Workers, American Unions.* 2d ed. Baltimore: Johns Hopkins University Press.

————. 1995. *The CIO, 1935–1945*. Chapel Hill: University of North Carolina Press.

Zilg, Gerard C. 1974. *Du Pont: Behind the Nylon Curtain*. Englewood Cliffs, N.J.: Prentice-Hall.

Zweigenhaft, Richard L., and G. William Domhoff. 1998. *Diversity in the Power Elite*. New Haven: Yale University Press.

INDEX

Entries followed by t *denote tables*